D1593503

The
ONE YEAR
Challenge

A new journey towards
LOVE, PURPOSE & COURTSHIP

KEREL R. PINDER

The
ONE YEAR
Challenge

A new journey towards
LOVE, PURPOSE & COURTSHIP

ISBN: 978-0-9847460-4-0
ISBN: 978-0-9847460-5-7 (ebook)

Design and Layout by Mr. Michael J. Matulka of Basik Studios
Omaha, Nebraska USA

Published by Basik Studios (*www.gobasik.com*)
Omaha, Nebraska USA

Printed in the USA

For all the amazing women and men
who decided to allow God to write their love story.

Acknowledgements

First I would like to thank God for His amazing hand in my life. I truly appreciate the gift He has given me through writing. I am also grateful for the blessing of losing my full time job six months ago and the covering He provided for me every step of the way. For if it wasn't for this season I may have never had the opportunity to tell my story.

To my parents; Peter and Joyce Pinder thank you for being my rock of support and a great source of wisdom. To my siblings Kenton and Katheldra thank you for being my backbone, my cheerleaders and most of all my friends.

To my first round of editors Katheldra, Grace and Mia, thank you for devoting your time to this project. Your wisdom and insight truly influenced the pages of this book. I genuinely appreciate you.

To all the men and women whose stories are woven through the pages of this book. Whether you entered my life for reason, season or lifetime, I am who I am today because of my time spent with you. So I want to truly say thank you for impacting my life in such a special way.

To my photographer Alfred Anderson thank you for always being my creative springboard. To my publishing team at Basik Studios, especially Michael & Sharrana Matulka, thank you for believing in my vision and helping me to package my purpose to present to the world.

Last but not least thank you, to YOU! You who believed in me enough to purchase this book, read my words and even read this acknowledgement page that most people love to skip over! THANK YOU!

Table of Contents

Preface

On January 9th, 2015, *The New York Times* published Mandy Len Catron's article "To Fall in Love With Anyone Do This..." In this article, Mandy gave a personal account of her experience with Dr. Aron's Study. For those who may not know, Dr. Aron's study was created more than twenty years ago to create interpersonal closeness between two strangers. These strangers were instructed to ask each other 36 questions followed by a four minute stare. Although this study sounds well in theory, like most people, I had my reservations. However, Mandy explained that she began to believe it worked when she learned from the study that one of the couples fell in love and got married six months later. Mandy then thought to herself, this just may be worth trying.

Mandy kept this theory in her mind and had the opportunity to share it with a colleague she was spending time with, at a bar one night. In the midst of conversation, he asked her, "I suspect, given a few commonalities, you could fall in love with anyone. If so, how do you choose someone?" This was when Mandy mentioned the study. To her surprise at that moment her colleague told her, "We should try it!" The rest of the article goes on to explain their connection through the questions and the emotions that were quickly building during the process. At the end of the article Mandy blissfully shared, that it worked. That night they fell in love.

In the article Mandy tried to caution readers that the 36 questions helped her to fall in love but she believed it worked because of several reasons. They both had an interest in each other before the 36 questions. Mandy also says they probably would have eventually fallen in love without the questions; this experiment simply seemed to speed up the process. However it didn't matter what cautions she gave, the message was out there – these 36 questions worked!

In her Ted-ex presentation, Mandy explained that she was not ready for the quick increase in fame that she and her new relationship were experiencing. Like most bloggers, Mandy's regular traffic stayed around the 250 to 500 views. However in a matter of days of her *New York Times* debut, Mandy's traffic increased to over 5,000 views and eventually it was over 57,000. Within two days, *The Today Show* and *Good Morning America* had both called her for interviews and by the end of the week Mandy's *New York Times* article had received over eight million views. It was clear that Mandy's love life was rapidly becoming the 'prototype'.

Mandy had no clue that she would experience such instant fame. She became overwhelmed by the increasing calls and emails that went on for weeks. Everyone with the same polarizing question, "Are you still in love?" People wanted to know if the study worked. Mandy felt this was too much pressure for a very new and growing relationship, so she turned down every interview. She wanted to protect her relationship from becoming idolized, to keep the authenticity of what she and her partner shared. She didn't want to be the prototype.

You see, Mandy stumbled upon this study while she was going through a tough breakup. Her heart kept overruling her mind during her previous relationship and now that it was over, she wanted to learn a 'smarter' way to love. Being the intellect that she was, Mandy turned to science. However she never expected the study to actually work, but it did. In efforts to once again caution love hopefuls, she explained in her Ted-x presentation, the reason she feels she is still in love today is because she makes a choice every day to stay in love.

Mandy says asking the questions are the easy part. It's staying in love every day after that determines the results of your relationship. She admitted that she had a young man come up to her at a school and tell her that he tried her study and that it didn't work. She asked him if he felt closer to the person after asking the questions, in which he replied "Yes!" She told him, "Well then it did work because the study was created to form interpersonal closeness, not help you fall in love."

I'm sure this isn't the answer he wanted, but it was the truth. We are the microwave to instant messages generation, so we want results, and we want them quick. Tell me you didn't Google the 36 questions within the first few paragraphs of reading this book. If you didn't Google them yet, most of you, if even just for a second, most likely contemplated with who and when you would try this study. And if you did, it's ok! We are designed for relationships. And we want to find love, and not just love, but lasting love.

In January 2013, like Mandy, I was going through a really difficult breakup, but instead of turning to science, I turned to Christ. Just one month prior, I was introduced to Andy Stanley's ONE YEAR CHALLENGE. A complete year with absolutely NO DATING! The challenge is created to help those who have spent years dating their way and are now willing to try it God's way. However, to date God's way, He would need some time to re-introduce you to the person He created you to be, hence the ONE year challenge. So I spent that year allowing God to transform me from the inside out. I was taking my love life out of my hands and allowing God to re-write my love story.

A few weeks after my year challenge had ended, I felt God tell me to write a book about my experience. At that time, I constantly questioned God, telling Him my story wasn't quite where I wanted it to be yet, and kept pushing it off. At the time, I didn't realize it, but I was telling God, "I need to wait until I can be the 'prototype.'" I wanted to remind God that people responded to prototypes. Mandy's story got picked up by *The New York Times* because she used the 36 questions and fell in love. *The Today Show* and *Good Morning America* called Mandy for an interview because they wanted to know if she was still in love. We love to see results! We want and need a prototype to believe that something is worth it.

God then told me, "I don't want you to be a prototype. I just want you to tell your story." Sigh. God wasn't getting it. Totally confused by His reasoning, I took an entire year to begin writing. You see in today's society, we follow Christian women like Heather Lindsay because she is transparent, down to earth, relatable and on fire for God. But, if we are honest, a lot of us also follow her or began to follow her because she was our 'prototype'. Heather's blogs, books and teachings tell us all about how she had a messed up past, sleeping with random guys, then she turned to God, didn't kiss her husband until her wedding day and boom, Perfect life! Heather is gorgeous, she has a gorgeous husband and two gorgeous children and her full-time job is to travel the world sharing a real talk about Jesus and how he saved her from all her mess. Seriously after following her Instagram for five minutes, I was like, "YESSSS sign me up. How do I get your life?"

Still, what God wanted to remind me of, is "Yes, I am using Heather, and I have blessed her, but Kerel, she is NOT your prototype. She is simply a messenger." God wants us to stop getting distracted by the desire to be the example and get more focused on simply delivering the message.

So although Mandy may have seemed crazy to turn down interviews from some of the most popular morning shows in America, Mandy got it right. She was NOT the prototype, and she wasn't trying to be. Heather Lindsay is not the prototype. Your best friend who slept with her boyfriend and still got the ring is not the prototype either. If you are on a search to find the kind of love that lasts, the kind of love that is unconditional, Christ is the only prototype, and He is the ONLY example we should be following.

Christ hid me behind the veil and made it possible for me to tell my story. He took a very broken woman and showed me what true love is. In *The One Year Challenge – A New Journey to Love, Purpose and Courtship*, I give a very transparent look into my journey. The relationships and experiences that led me to take a year off from dating, the ups and downs of what that year was like and the restoration God brought to my life in the end. So when you read the upcoming pages of my motivational memoir, remember I am NOT the prototype. I am simply a girl who was led to share her story and the lessons God taught me along the way. My story takes some unexpected twists and turns, and it may not even have the ending you expected, but it's exactly the way my story was meant to be written.

REVELATION

CHAPTER 1

Love is Not Always a Fairytale

I remember playing hopscotch in the sixth grade. One of the most popular girls in our class was giving us the 411 on relationships. As usual, we all listened attentively as if she was giving us the gospel of truth. I have no idea who decides who is 'popular' and who isn't in primary school. Regardless of what it was, I knew she was "popular" and I wasn't and in primary school being "popular" will somehow make you the authority on everything! So I listened. She went on to tell us that her mom said girls who have a lot of boyfriends in high school usually don't get married as early as the ones who don't. Hmmm, by this time I never even had a boyfriend, so I thought that I was in pretty good shape.

However in retrospect, it's a little unsettling that this prediction scared me so much. Here I was in the sixth grade worrying about when I would get married. When my obsessions should have been what the lunch lady was serving for lunch that day or which Backstreet Boy I thought was cute. On the contrary, I wasn't thinking about any of that, I was too busy cringing at the fact that I could be one of those ladies that didn't get married early. Why did I care so much? I still have no clue why at that age, this fear crippled me so much, but it did. Maybe it was the disappointment of never being chosen to play the 'mommy' when all of the kids were playing house, or the rejection I felt during catching kisses. It didn't matter how slow I ran, no boy ever tried to catch me. I have no idea what form of rejection pierced the root of my developing insecurity, all I knew is that the pain was starting to grow. So I decided, like my mother, a ring would be on my finger by my early twenties. You see my mother got engaged during her senior year of college, and I felt there was no reason I couldn't follow suit. At least that's what I thought....

My First Love

Unfortunately, my luck with the guys in high school didn't prove to be that exciting either. I had one to two week 'relationships' here and there matched with crushes that lasted for years on end but nothing concrete. So maybe if my primary school friend's theory was correct, I was right where I needed to be.

Just as I began to give up on my very own teenage love affair, Cupid decided to send his arrow my way during my senior year of high school. Every year when school started, I would look forward to fresh faces, thinking maybe this will be my year to meet someone new and every year I was greeted with the same fate: absolutely nobody! However, this year proved to be different. That year some students that passed their 12th grade national exams in the 10th and 11th grade were able to go on to a Jumpstart program. This program involved other 12th grade students from various high schools throughout the island attending our local college in order to receive college credits. Excited to be chosen, I had no idea how much this opportunity would change my life.

Currently, I am outgoing and fun-loving, but in high school I was quite shy. My best friend at the time was very outgoing and popular with a very polarizing personality. So naturally she took the role of the extrovert and I was the unassuming introvert in our duo. She always knew how to get the attention of everyone and I often spent most of my high school years in her shadow. I knew I was dynamic on my own but for some reason I never really got to shine when she was by my side. However, this time would prove to be different.

I remember it like yesterday. It was a warm day in September when I looked up, and his gaze met mine, was he looking at me? In retrospect, in high school, I had very shallow taste in what I looked for in a guy and for the first time, my list was sitting right in front of me. A cream colored man with a radiant smile, I was in heaven. And even better than that, he was looking right at me. No standing in the shadow this time, at sixteen I thought this could be it!

Every class we would share coy glances and a subtle flirtatious banter, in my mind it was the making of something beautiful, until my best friend busted my bubble at the first parent meeting. I said to her I think he's cute, in which she replied, "Who him? You know he has a girlfriend right? Yeah the girl sitting next to him, that's his girlfriend. So I hope you're not thinking anything will happen between you and him, so just forget about it." I thought to myself, "Great, after years of standing in the shadow, someone FINALLY notices ME, and now he has a girlfriend, just my luck." I kept a friendly distance. I respected the fact that he had a girlfriend and never physically acted on emotions while they were together. However emotionally my feelings began to evolve, every time we spoke on MSN messenger my butterflies grew stronger. (Yes, for those of you who went to high school in the 90's and early 00's, MSN messenger was the main form of communication, before Facebook was invented.)

It was clear he wasn't happy with his relationship, but I could never ask him to leave. If he left her because I asked him to, I would always stand in fear that one day he would do the same thing to me. So I kept my boundaries, but still flirted every chance I got. After a few weeks of getting to know each other, he told me the news I had been waiting for since the day we met, he was finally going to leave her. In my excitement, I tried to remain calm and level headed, making sure he wasn't just leaving her for me, but leaving because he wasn't happy in the relationship anymore. He assured me that he made this decision because he knew he didn't want to be in that relationship anymore. In fact, now that he was single, he thought it might be best just to be single for a while. "WHAT!! Wait that's not a part of the plan." I didn't want him to leave his girlfriend for me, but I also didn't want him to fall in love with this new found freedom that involved him entertaining any other girls. I had to think quickly; this new found interest was ending before it even started.

He then asked me if I was ok with the fact that he just wanted to 'do him' for a while. He had been a relationship for so long he just wanted some time to experience being single in high school. Hindsight is 20/20 because when I look back at this statement, I realize that it was the first red flag of what was to come. Take note here: if a guy says he wants something, don't try to convince him to do anything else. Chances are he knows what he can handle. However, at sixteen I had never had a 'real' boyfriend. I never had someone to fill my shallow rooted checklist who was so interested in me, and I wasn't ready to throw all that away. As a child, I had always been very strong willed and at times I can be very adamant about getting my way. So I said, "Sure that's fine, do what you have to do," in that "you better NOT do what you have to do" tone. He then said to me, "Really?? And you'll wait for me until I'm ready to date again?" "The heck I won't," I replied. I assured him that taking the time to be single was a choice he had to make. I would have to live with it if he made the choice to be single, but I definitely wouldn't be sitting around waiting until he finished sowing his royal oats.

In his attempt NOT to lose out on what could have been a beautiful thing between us, he forfeited his desire to experience the single life in high school and decided to make me his girl. Victory!! I was over the moon. I was about to enter into my first real relationship. In retrospect, I realize that this was the first time I used manipulation to get what I wanted, and that was the first time he lied to himself. We didn't realize what we started, but time would soon tell what was about to unfold...

My First Teenage Love Affair

The next few weeks were simply heaven. We would have frequent 'study' sessions at my house. Because we didn't attend the same school, it allowed us to see each other more frequently outside of the Jumpstart program. I had waited years to know what it felt like to be in a real relationship and believe me the feeling was so great! I spent Christmas with his family and had flowers laid out for me on the seat of his car when he picked me up from school on Valentine's Day. Years before, I watched the girls in my class get showered with flowers, teddy bears and chocolates and this year it was finally me. This year I had a big teddy bear and chocolate sitting in the back seat of his dad's car waiting for me. The years spent waiting to know what this was like was worth it, I was finally in 'love.'

Of course, the aftermath with the ex-girlfriend left us on eggshells for a while. In the beginning, we decided to be private about our relationship to avoid it getting messy. Eventually, she discovered the truth and labeled me as a 'home wrecker' and a clear enemy in her eyes. This dynamic was not going to be pretty, but luckily catty remarks behind my back were as far as it went.

The real fire didn't hit the fan until the end of February during our senior year. Everyone that was a part of the Junior Achievement program went to Nassau for their annual conference. I wasn't in the program but I was in Nassau at the same time for a swim meet, so I still got to see my boyfriend, just not every night. When I came back to school after the weekend, the rumors spread like wildfire, everyone said that my boyfriend slept with another girl on the trip, I thought this couldn't be true. It was just two weeks after experiencing the best Valentine's Day ever. Just so you know in the twelfth grade, a teddy bear and chocolates calculated as the best Valentine's Day ever. I couldn't believe what I was hearing. The girl they were claiming he was with, was in the same class as me for goodness sake. He wouldn't be that disrespectful, would he?

My girls assured me I couldn't ask him directly for the truth, he would easily lie, or worse flip the script on me. So our weekly study session quickly turned into a CSI unit, little did I know this was the planting of my first 'psycho' antics. We called everyone we knew that was on that trip to try and discover the truth. No one wanted to admit that they knew what happened. They kept referring us to someone else; this merry go round was getting us nowhere. I finally got fed up and decided to give him a call. He said to me with a stern voice after I said hello, "So are you done with your little investigation?" "What?? Did he know? How could he? Who told??" I felt betrayed by the persons who had no information in the first place, what the hell? I felt defeated.

He expressed his disappointment at my lack of trust and immaturity by calling everybody that I didn't know. He said I should have talked to him and asked him for the truth, "Because the truth was that he would never cheat on me." Oh, he was good, he was really good, he was 'flipping the script on me' and I didn't even know it. In that one minute, he won me over. From that day on, it would be me and him against the world, the next Bonnie and Clyde. I roll my eyes and cringe every time I think of how naive and gullible I was at the time. When your worth is wrapped up in a relationship, more than it's wrapped up in Christ, you accept what you want to hear instead of accepting the truth. I convinced myself that everyone was spreading the rumors because they wanted to 'destroy' us. What we didn't realize is that we were already destroying ourselves. He was building his lies, and my insecurities were beginning to take root.

From that day on I bought his lies and defended my man with a badge of honor. I went up to the girl, who supposedly saw everything, at school the next day. I told her, "Tell me to my face what you saw, since you saw something." She denied seeing anything; she probably looked at me and knew I had already made up my mind. She knew I saw him as innocent and that there was probably nothing she could say to make me think otherwise. So she let me walk away in my false sense of comfort.

She had known that I was a naive little girl who would believe only what she wanted to believe and right then and there, I only wanted to believe that he was innocent. So to me, he was.

Eventually, the rumors died down, and our budding romance began to grow again. However, the movie dates, long walks on the beach and Saturdays in his dad's swimsuit store listening to Bob Marley were about to come to an end. We would be heading to college in the fall, and my mom was not interested in me attending our local college in the Bahamas in efforts to 'stay with my man'. She insisted that Canada would be a great choice. And at the time, he and I believed that love would conquer all, so we decided on the long distance option instead of breaking up.

We spent almost every day of that summer together, visiting the dolphins, taking long drives throughout the island and sometimes just watching TV together. We soaked up every moment as it was about to be a long four months. My first week at school I cried like a baby, and it wasn't because I missed my mom and dad, was homesick or wanted some Bahamian food. I simply just missed my boyfriend. I remember showing up to one of the older girls' dorm rooms in tears because I didn't have a phone card, and I just wanted to call my boyfriend. My room had pictures we had taken over the last year. Most people go to college and can't wait to be free; I went to college and spent every night dreaming about my high school sweetheart. That Christmas when my dad picked me up from the airport, I exclaimed well you know where the first stop has to be. My dad scolded me for being so 'giddy' and that I should at least go home and get settled first. I pouted the whole way home until I saw him.

The next semester, we continued to conquer our way through the ups and downs of a long distance relationship. Time together was always an "up" and time apart proved to be a "down". Cheating rumors surfaced from time to time, but again I stood 'behind my man'. After my first summer home, we shared one of the best summers of my life. It was the summer I became a 'woman'. We were older, had a little more freedom and were still madly in love. However at the end of that summer when it was time to return to school, we both had a real conversation about how hard it was to remain faithful while apart. At the time, we were eighteen and nineteen year-old teenagers. We committed to knowing that we would want to marry each other once we finished college. However, we both felt we owed it to each other to give the other a chance to explore what was out there before settling down. We didn't want to end up doing something that we would regret. Little did I know, he had already done something that he regretted. This pact made him feel less guilty about stepping out because he was 'nice' enough to give me the opportunity to 'sow my royal oats' as well.

So when I began my sophomore year, I started to hang out with a male friend in secret. Admitting to my friends that I was in an open relationship and just hanging out with one of our male friends from time to time called for too much of an explanation. This situation was more than I was ready to explain. I wasn't sleeping with him, so I knew their response would have been "well then what's the point?" I just wanted the company, and I needed to be in an open relationship to NOT feel guilty about this emotional connection. So I kept the fact that I was spending time with this guy to myself.

At the end of the semester, I had a fight with the guy I was dating and when my friends found out, they were furious because they didn't even know that I was even dating someone. They then surprisingly insisted that my secrecy is what had me in the situation I was in right then. I didn't understand what they meant. What situation was I in? They had apparently known that my boyfriend back home was ALWAYS cheating on me. They went on to say that all the rumors I heard about my boyfriend from the time I came to school were ALL true. He was always cheating on me. They even knew one of the girl's personally, but never told me because they watched me chew out anyone who told me that he was stepping out on me. They figured I would never believe them so they never saw the point of telling me. However that night, my opening up about the guy I was secretly dating gave them the conviction to finally be straight with me.

I think this was the first time in my life that emotional pain hit me so hard that it physically began to hurt my body. I had a final exam the next day, and here I was in a group study room of the school's library having all of my dreams ripped at the seams. My first love, the guy I shared my heart, body and soul with, the man who I planned to marry one day was a liar…

Have you ever had your heart broken? I'm not even quite sure how to describe it. I just know the pain rips at your core and at times you feel like you can barely breathe, and that's what I felt like that day. The tears began to roll down my face, and I began to scream uncontrollably, for the first time since that day in high school in my friend's bedroom I knew I heard the truth. Today I can still see myself so vividly lying on the library floor gasping for breath through my tears. Anyone who would have passed would have sworn someone had just died.

The crazy thing is, something did die, and it was a part of me. Without me even knowing it, a little piece of me died that day. It was the piece of me that believed that love had a happy ending, or that trust was the foundation of any solid relationship. That day I built a wall inside so I would never trust or love that freely again. I got home and ripped the photos off the wall and threw the frames to the ground like a crazy person. My friend yanked my headphones out of my ears and gave me a really good shaking and demanded I snap out of this. I had started listening to Toni Braxton's song 'Unbreak My Heart', and something in me snapped, I just sat there confused wondering, how could he betray me like this?

Of course when I called him later that night he denied everything. So again like a private eye, I began to call all over the Bahamas from Canada trying to get to the bottom of it all. The girl from high school's story resurfaced with all the others. I demanded that he call her so that I could confront them both about their deceit. Instead, they both chastised me over a three-way call. She asked me why I was wasting her time with an almost two-year-old rumor. She exclaimed, "How many times do I have to tell you that story is not true, you need to get a life and stop being so insecure!" Funny thing is before this moment, I never really felt that insecure. However at that moment, I felt childhood insecurities begin to seep into my spirit and take root in my soul once again. I went quiet on the phone, but I no longer believed him or her. The roots of my insecurity quickly turned into branches. Trust became a figment of the imagination. As far as I was concerned, trust in relationships didn't exist anymore.

We didn't end our relationship on the phone that day because I refused to walk away without hearing him tell me the truth. So in a week's time, I was home in the Bahamas for Christmas, and that's when the investigation went from phone calls to emails. A girlfriend of mine was dating my boyfriend's friend at the time, and she told me the password to my boyfriend's computer was my name. So that's when the email stalking junky was born, calling people to get to the truth did me no good in the past, and it wouldn't do me any good now. If his email password was the same as his computer we would be as they say in the Bahamas 'cooking with gas' and sure enough it was!

All of the proof was finally in the pudding. I called him and told him we needed to talk, he said he wouldn't be coming home for Christmas but would be there for New Years, so I waited. The day he came in, we went to the beach we often frequented and I told him everything I knew. "I read the emails, and I found out about two other women, so tell me the truth. I've heard a million rumors about you, so I need to know, did you ever cheat on me and if so with who?" He didn't look at me right away; I don't think he could. He stared out at the ocean with a solemn and defeated look on his face. His eyes were bloodshot red; he was tired of running. We had shared two ½ years together, and this is how it was about to end. He sighed and said, "Every story you ever heard about me is true."

I couldn't believe my ears. Everything was true! I had a feeling some of it was true, but hearing that all of it was true was something I just wasn't ready to hear. I started to name names, and with every name he shamefully shook his head. I spent the last two ½ years thinking that I had found my soul mate, but I was sharing it with someone who constantly lied to my face. He lied to me and then made me feel guilty every time I would ask him about it. I felt sick. He pleaded for another chance, but I couldn't. It wasn't just a kiss; it wasn't even just one girl. It was some girls I knew, girls who I passed by in parties and never understood what their sorrowful looks meant. They were watching the guy they slept with every night, parade "the wife" around when they knew where he would be later that night. It hurt like a ton of bricks to walk away, but I felt as if I had no choice. To excuse all of those forms of betrayal would make me a fool, so I had to walk away.

He spent several months trying to win me back, but I couldn't look at him the same way anymore. So eventually he started to date again and in that moment I felt like I wanted to die. How was he moving on before me? I don't care if he begged me to get back together for almost a year; he couldn't move on before I did, right? Well, he could, and he did. When someone hurts you, a part of you wants 'justice' to prevail as long as it can. You want to see them alone, hurt and incapable of moving on without you because that's how they made you feel. However, that's not forgiveness, and that's not love. The opposite of love isn't hatred; it's indifference. I was still in love with him, but I had no idea what to do with all of these feelings.

Often as women, we allow what we want to blind us from what we are worth and deserve.

My self-worth was still wrapped up in his acceptance, and I was drowning. Often as women, we allow what we want to blind us from what we are worth and deserve. I knew I deserved more. Unfortunately, I couldn't bring myself to demand more. So despite the fact that he moved on, when summers and Christmas vacations came, and I was back home in the Bahamas, our connection proved to withstand the test the time. At times, I became the other woman that he was 'stealing love' with on the side. I made myself feel less guilty by convincing myself I was paying back all the women who helped him betray me years ago for the pain they caused me. However I was fooling myself, these were different women, and I was now different too. I was creating a downward spiral of insecurity, selfishness, and low self-esteem that was killing the innocence inside of me.

Eventually one Christmas a few years later, we were both home and for the first time since we had broken up, we were both single at the same time. So I decided to revisit the topic of getting back together. We had not officially been together for three years, but our times together proved our love had not died. However, surprisingly that night, he assured me that the ship had sailed and that we would only ever be friends. Again I was devastated. I thought we had a connection, so how could he be so sure? We were only 21 at the time. At eighteen he told me he would marry me when I was 21. "Can we rewind to the fact that you were the one who cheated on me and then begged me to take you back for almost a year?" I tried to cling for dear life to a relationship God had tried to release me from years ago. Rejection can be the coldest bruise to an ego. It grows trees of insecurity and by now, my tree had leaves!

So there I was 21 years old, months into working my first real job and the only man I ever really loved told me it was over. My childhood plan of being married by 21 was looking pretty bleak. I was like my favorite character Joan from the TV show, Girlfriends and like Joan, my timeline had expired, and there was no man in sight. I was officially starting over.

The Root of it All

I had harbored this fairytale dream for so long. I didn't realize that from the time I was young, I nursed these expectations in my heart, blinded to all of the signs that kept telling me to walk away from unhealthy relationships. Accepting Christ means turning your will over to Him. However, when I met my first love, turning my will over to God was the last thing on my mind. I acknowledged God, went to church every Sunday but having a relationship with Him where His will came before mine was simply unfathomable.

I always thought it was so simple: you meet a good guy, you fall in love, you get married and then you have children, right? I saw it happen for so many other people. Why wasn't the fairytale happening for me? I never knew being sold out to Christ was a part of the equation. I know some of you may think the same thing. We all know a lot of people who are married and never decided to be sold out to Christ. But, as God told me, when you have a call on your life, you can't watch what God is doing in the lives of others. You have to simply trust the timing of what He is doing in yours. God loved me so much that He saved me from myself, not just once but over and over again.

Unfortunately going through the pain of losing my first love didn't wake me up to the reality that God won't bless a mess. So I continued to drag myself through messy situations, searching to find wholeness and completion through a relationship. Either no one ever told me or I never realized that the real meaning of life wasn't to make it to the day when someone said "And they both lived happily ever after." I had to learn the hard way; love isn't always a fairytale.

Growth Exercise:

1. What childhood memories have helped to shape your current outlook on relationships and life?

2. What is your idea of 'Happily Ever After'? Do you think your idea is realistic or a fairytale?

Chapter 2

Man's Rejection is God's Protection

Often when I hear the phrase, "Man's rejection is God's protection" it reminds me of when I did swim lessons with my godchild. After a few lessons, she was convinced that she could swim on her own. After watching her technique, I knew that she hadn't put everything together yet to be able to hold herself above water. She, however, believed she knew better than me. She constantly cried for me to let her go, screaming she could do it on her own, and that she was ready. I fought her tooth and nail. I knew she wasn't ready, and I knew if I let her go on her own she would drown. Despite my warnings, she continued to protest. So eventually I let her go, and down she went. She bubbled, gasping for breath, desperately stretching her hands toward me so that I could save her. Sound familiar? This controlling spirit is what we try to force upon Christ.

We learn a few lessons, pass a few tests and all of sudden we are ready to tell God that we know what to do. God my 'Adam' should be here, I am ready! When God goes silent or tells us not yet, we sometimes still do it. It's not until we realize that we are drowning that we are willing to admit that God was right. God told us not to go into the water by ourselves to protect us, not to punish us. I often let my goddaughter bubble for a few seconds so that she could understand what I meant when I said she wasn't ready; I honestly believe sometimes God does this to us as well. He allows men to reject us, for our protection.

After my 'fairytale' ended with my first love, I had my fair share of rejection in relationships, but out of all those relationships there was one experience that stuck out like a sore thumb. I had a powerful romance with a guy that I was once again convinced was going to be the 'one'. From the moment we began to get to know one another, the compliments flowed like water. He was what I needed to boost my self-esteem and little did I know I was what he needed to boost his. However, there was one problem; he had a girlfriend. I couldn't believe it; it was like I was a magnet for unavailable men. Lesson learned: the devil doesn't have any new tricks!

Spiritually, it seemed my brokenness kept attracting broken men. However once again to 'try' and remain respectful, I told him not to leave her because of me, leave her because you're unhappy. I realized later that this line was a comforting lie that I told myself to make myself feel less guilty. The truth was, it didn't matter that I never went on a date, saw or touched him while he was in a relationship. The fact that I provided a listening ear to his problems made me an available out. An available out that would soon learn that karma can be a real pain in the butt. I was helping him emotionally cheat on his girlfriend, and I was just as much to blame as he was.

Eventually, he left his relationship. I then tried everything in my power to advise him to take some time to himself to get over the relationship. However, he assured me that he was over it and knew what he wanted and what he wanted was me. At this time, I had little to no self-esteem, so this line was all I needed to be hooked. The first few months were just what I needed too. He had a way with words that assured me that I was the woman of his dreams. This helped to fill my desperate need for approval and love. It even came complete with a spiritual devotion every morning during the first few months of dating; it was complete bliss.

One day during Sunday dinner, he boldly told my father we would soon be giving him the grandchildren that he always wanted because it wouldn't be long before he married me! "WHAT!! YES!!" I was beyond excited! I knew it was all moving a little fast but when you know, you just know, right? My friends told me time and time again, "Why rush, you're still young, you guys seem to be moving so fast." I told them they just didn't understand we were in love, and that's all that mattered. Well, at least that's what I thought...

Eventually the morning devotions stopped, the date nights and outings turned into sitting on the couch for the whole weekend and we began to have arguments about the silliest things. One day while I thought we were having a normal day shopping, he snapped at me mid-conversation and asked why I was always so giddy? "What?" Everyone who knows me knew that I have always been a ball of energy. He found it cute and endearing when we first met, now he simply found it annoying. What was going on here?

A word to the wise, if a guy/girl is in a serious relationship and was hurt in the process, dating them right after makes you a possible rebound. What's the rebound you may ask? The overwhelming amount of gratitude they shower you with in the beginning for just being 'you', is probably their need to see someone in a better light. When you return with words of affirmation, it simply serves as the self-esteem booster that they need after getting out of a relationship that may have caused their self-esteem to fall.

As a caution, please note that they honestly may not be aware that they are doing it. It's just a matter of survival for them. Getting over a relationship on your own is really difficult. Therefore as the rebound, without knowing it you are serving as the pacifier they need until their self-esteem is reassured enough within themselves to get back on their feet. Once they're back on their feet, the reality of what your relationship is may no longer be what they need. You were there to serve as a self-esteem booster, and now that you have boosted their self-esteem, there is no longer a need for you. Sad but true!

I fell in love with being in love and the process, instead of evaluating if I ever really loved myself.

Needless to say a few months later, the second man that I thought I was going to marry was slipping away. The man who bought me flowers the first time he met me in person and sent me sweet cards 'just because it was Thursday' finally got back on his feet. I was no longer what he needed. However, I couldn't only blame him. The signs that he was not ready to be in a relationship were there from the beginning. But my low self-esteem that started when I was younger and morphed me into a young woman with a marriage timeline blindsided me. So I ignored the signs. The insecurities from being repeatedly cheated on and then rejected played in my mind. I found comfort in being with a guy who said he wanted to marry me, without being alert to the warning signs. I placed marriage on a pedestal and made it my conquest. I fell in love with being in love and the process, instead of evaluating if I ever really loved myself.

It's funny how moments of pain still play so vividly in your mind. I can remember the weekend we broke up as if it was yesterday. Three days of planned bliss turned into an argument after every five minutes. Everything came to a head on the Saturday night when he went out with his friends and didn't come back until 3 a.m. He admitted he stayed out late as a way to punish me for the argument we had earlier in the day. As each hour passed that night, my anger fueled even more, I couldn't believe my relationship was falling apart right before my eyes. In retrospect, I realize that when I was faced with loneliness and rejection that is when God was calling me back to Him.

The hurtful part is that I did try to end it, before it got this far. Weeks before, when he called me annoying, I suggested we call it quits. I didn't know a lot about myself, but I did know I had a jovial personality, and if that was going to be annoying to him, maybe we didn't have a shot. We were arguing so much I wanted to give him a way out, but he said no. We were just having a rough time, but now this was no longer a rough time, this was clearly the end. When he came home, he asked what I was still doing up. "What am I still doing up? What do you think I'm doing up, having the sudden urge to catch up on reruns of *Girlfriends*! No, you idiot, I'm waiting for you!" At this point, the argument couldn't even get louder. I had no energy, and we were fighting a losing battle. But even in my darkest moments, God was still with me every step of the way.

If you have ever wrung out a wet towel, you would notice that you have to squeeze it over and over in your hands, turning every end until all the water is gone. I believe that's what God does to us sometimes. He stretches us and squeezes us until all the water is gone. The water falls from the wet towel, similarly to how the tears fall from our eyes and although the process is painful, like that towel we would never be completely dry without this process. God counts our tears, and I believe he allows us to go through certain storms so that we can be shaped and molded into who He called us to be.

We were two broken souls trying to find comfort in each other instead of learning to find comfort in Christ.

I sat on my boyfriend's kitchen counter at four a.m. and as we looked into each other's eyes, we both knew that this was the end. We were over and if we were honest with ourselves we never even really had a chance. He never really loved me, he loved the idea of what we could be and I loved the idea that someone wanted to marry me. We were two broken souls trying to find comfort in each other instead of learning to find comfort in Christ. I cried out to God so much because I couldn't understand the pain that came with being rejected once again.

By the time the relationship was over, my tree of insecurity had grown even taller and the pieces of my broken heart were falling all over again. I knew I needed time alone, so this time I took it. However instead of healing, I spent the whole time convincing myself that time alone would bring us back together. I don't even understand why I thought it would be better the second time, but my self-esteem couldn't handle the idea that another guy didn't want to be with me.

I wanted to focus on developing a better me, but somewhere down the road my obsession with marriage simply became dormant, instead of obsolete. I was still secretly nursing my pain. I would still ask mutual friends how he was doing, and I would stalk his Facebook page from time to time. Why was I doing this? What was going on in his life shouldn't have been any of my concern, but it was. Instead of chopping my tree of insecurity completely down, I simply trimmed the leaves. Months later he had clearly moved on, and I had to learn to do the same.

However I struggled for a long time, trying to get over this relationship, wondering why God wouldn't allow it to work. God showed me that even though we can try to maneuver or fix whatever we want, He will always have the final say. Anything God wants to happen will happen. Things don't just manifest by happenstance; God is orchestrating the scenes of your life. When you are begging for an old relationship, and no matter how hard you try, you can't seem to make it work, it's because God is hiding you, He's shielding you, and He is desperately trying to protect you.

I remember calling my ex a little while after we ended our relationship only for him to tell me, "I'm in the middle of something, I'll call you right back," he never did. The funny thing is, I would actually sit there waiting and believing that he actually would. I didn't understand how I got there at the time, but God did. God was using the rejection, pain and depression to press me into new seasons of my life; He was just waiting for me to accept it. God showed me that when he presses His hand against you, it's because He wants to birth something inside of you. He doesn't want you to run away from the anointing. He wants you to use it to fuel your purpose. When I became discouraged, God surrounded me with stories of others who overcame rejection and received God's protection. Knowing that someone else made it through helped to restore my hope.

Pain into Purpose

When I think of someone who used rejection to fuel their purpose, my mind immediately goes to Sarah Jakes Roberts, the daughter of Mega Pastor Bishop T.D. Jakes. If you haven't read her testimony, I strongly encourage you to purchase her book *Lost and Found*. In this personal memoir, Sarah bravely tells her story of how she got pregnant at the age of thirteen. Sarah spent the next few years dealing with rejection from her peers and other church members. This led her into a broken marriage that eventually ended in divorce.

She tried to clean up her mistakes, but only made them worse. Sarah's story reminded me of the many times I tried to 'fix' my life by doing things my way instead of listening to God's way. Sarah eventually found her purpose when she started writing her blog. She was no longer ashamed of her past because she realized that her pain would birth her purpose. She eventually launched her first book and began speaking all over the world on her message of God's redemption. Sarah allowed man's rejection to be God's protection when she stopped believing what people said about her and started to believe who God said she was: fearfully and wonderfully made.

I once heard a psychologist say that you base your self-worth on what you believe the most important person in your life thinks about you. Your worth is determined by what they say, how they feel and act toward you. Reading Sarah's story reminded me of how I unknowingly made my boyfriends into quasi-gods, they were my lifeline and when their words and actions didn't validate me, I felt insecure, anxious and impatient for security. When they no longer wanted to be with me, when they said words that hurt me, I believed that I was no longer worthy of being loved by anyone. When God is the most important person in your life, your self-worth will be wrapped up in Him. I've come to realize that when you believe what God says about you, you will always see yourself as worthy, accepted, approved, loved, redeemed, forgiven, confident and secure.

Today I thank God for not giving me what I begged for, because when I look at our lives now I can see how much we both were better off without each other. I was begging God to fix it when all He wanted to do was protect me from it. Romans 5:3-5 (NIV) tells us to "rejoice in suffering because suffering brings, perseverance, perseverance brings character and character brings hope." God showed me that the more you ignore the hope and vision that He has for your life, the longer you will take to heal.

Growth Exercise:

1. Search your heart and ask God to show you if there are any areas in your life that you are still trying to force or keep open.

2. Write down a memory of a time where God showed you that man's rejection was His protection over you.

Chapter 3
Hurt People, Hurt People

After taking some time to be alone, I began to capture a glimpse of the vision Christ had for my life. However instead of building on this vision and allowing God to heal me completely, I decided to run ahead of God's timing, before I ever completely learned how to crawl. I thought because I had spent six months focusing on something other than a relationship, God had fixed me.

So I began dating again and at first, it turned out to be one of the best relationships I ever had. We met on social media, which isn't as weird as it sounds because we were both living in the Bahamas and had a number of mutual friends. The crazy thing is I told a mutual friend that I had a crush on him a few years before he sent me a friend request, but we never got the chance to meet in person. During our first conversation we realized we had a whole lot in common. The sparks were definitely there. And our initial coy flirtation quickly bloomed into a great relationship, with a solid friendship as its foundation.

We were in sync and life was good. We were together for three and a half years; we traveled together, celebrated milestones together and most of all held each other's hand through life's

There was always a deep connection when we were together.

difficult blows. Whether we were at a fancy dinner or chilling in our pajamas, there was always a deep connection when we were together.

He became one of my biggest supporters and with my many obligations he was sometimes the only voice at the end of my cheering squad. I remember I was performing a dramatization at one of my many competitions and at this point everyone who had supported me over the years, was over it. So in a room filled with contestant's supporters I had one. He held my video camera in his hand and shouted from the back of the room in constant support. In that moment it didn't matter that I didn't have a room filled with hundreds of cheerleaders, because I had him. I had fallen in love with my best friend and I felt like I could honestly do life with him forever.

Our relationship wasn't perfect but for the most part I felt like we fit perfectly together. So I honestly don't think I can pinpoint the exact moment that this relationship took a turn for the worst. But if I had to choose, I would say that it was the day I blatantly decided to say NO to God.

I came to a crossroads in my relationship when my boyfriend suggested we part ways. He said that it wasn't because we didn't love each other but because the distance we were about to encounter could be a strain on our relationship. I rejected this suggestion and almost took it personally. Was he saying he no longer wanted to be with me? At that time, I couldn't see what he saw, and I couldn't see what God wanted me to see. Although we had a great relationship, it was often strained by my constant jealousy and insecurities. I never dealt with the pain from my previous relationships and therefore I would constantly accuse him of cheating or trying to leave me. I had finally found my "happy ending" and I tried to hold on as tight as I could. So I couldn't see the good in all of this, I desperately wanted to keep what was comfortable and familiar to me.

A few days before my boyfriend suggested we part ways, we were sitting in church together, and the choir was singing Shekinah Glory's, *Say Yes* and I felt God tell me "I need you to walk away from this relationship." I said, "God you have to kidding me, I finally found the man of my dreams and I must walk away!" Obviously I had only short term memory and forgot what distance could do to a relationship, even when two people are in love.

Needless to say, I ignored my boyfriend's suggestion and the prompting of the Holy Spirit that day. I had always had a dominant personality, and I wasn't about to lose this fight. I could do this. After a while, time would tell how wrong I truly was. As he had predicted, the long distance did prove to be a strain on our relationship. Time also proved that we were in two different chapters in our lives. I wanted to be married, and he was still trying to find himself. I wanted a family, and he couldn't even begin to think about one because he had to focus on his career. At the time, my selfish desires left me completely oblivious to the fact that I was only thinking about myself.

A few months later I brought the topic of marriage up, and I asked him to give me a time frame when he could see himself getting married. He told me right then and there after a year and a half of dating he knew for sure he wouldn't be ready for marriage for another five years. I wanted to die, WHAT??? Here I thought I was at least a year away from a ring, yet he was telling me five years. I then began to feel rejected all over again. I couldn't believe it, this should have been my queue to leave, but I didn't want to lose him. Don't get me wrong I shouldn't have left just because I wasn't getting my man-made timeline of being married by a certain age fulfilled. I should have walked away because he was honest enough to tell me, "We are not on the same page right now and if walking away is what you need to do, I will understand." Sometimes as women we believe we can change the way a man thinks when honestly the only person we can change is ourselves. In retrospect there were clearly written, billboard signs suggesting that I go the other way, the danger was ahead. But I kept listening to my selfish desires. I was going to make this work!

Playing for Keeps

Have you ever stayed somewhere when everything in you, was telling you it was time to go? Have you ever talked yourself out of leaving, because you felt that you invested too much time and too much energy to let it all go now? So despite your better judgment and the prompting of the Holy Spirit, you dig a bigger hole and decide to play for keeps.

Well at that moment we decided to do the same, we decided to play our hand. Totally oblivious to the fact that this was the day our seeds of our resentment for each other were beginning to grow. I resented him for telling me I would have to wait five more years, and I truly believe he resented me, for making him feel pressured about marriage when he wasn't even sure of the exact life he wanted for himself.

I believe it was then that we both dodged the signs that showed that we both equally wanted to walk away, but also equally wanted to try our best to fight and stay. You see we wanted to walk away because we were no longer on the same page and could no longer completely fulfill each other's happiness. But we didn't want to let go because our connection had been so deep. What if we never found that again with someone else or even worse what if we could never find it again with each other? I don't think either of us wanted to take that risk. So instead of risking it all, we played for keeps.

I kept his heart, and he kept mine, and we began to fight to hold on to the love we still held inside. We thought nothing is sadder than two people, who love each other, but just can't be together. However, I learned nothing is sadder than people who don't know the love of God and, therefore, truly cannot love themselves. So despite the fight to hold on, eventually without knowing it my resentment turned to frustration and then into anger.

> I learned nothing is sadder than people who don't know the love of God and, therefore, truly cannot love themselves.

This anger led to me eventually hurting my boyfriend. When he could no longer fulfill my emotional needs instead of turning to God, I turned to a male friend and began emotionally cheating on my boyfriend. In our society until something physical happens we disregard hanging out and flirting with someone else as cheating. However the truth is, if you are saying or doing something you could never do in front of your significant other, then you are already cheating.

The flirtation eventually led to a kiss, and that is when I realized I went too far. I know to some people unless you have sexual intercourse, you don't think you have gone too far, but being that intimate with someone when I was committed to someone else, for me was going too far. I tried to hide it at first but the deceit was growing inside me and beginning to burn at my core. I spent so much time ignoring the red flags that my flirtatious banter would eventually get me in trouble, that I missed the signs that led me on to the other side of full betrayal. I refused to heal after being broken and rejected so many times, so I made excuses for my behavior until I was out of excuses and had to be real with my truth.

After a lot of suspicious behavior my boyfriend knew I was hiding something from him, so I eventually admitted my truth, hoping he would understand and in some warped reality hoping I was right about the trust issues I displayed with him. Foolishly wishing he also had some skeletons hidden that would cancel both of our debts, leaving us both with the opportunity to start over. However there was nothing for him to confess, it was only me who was to blame. I spent so much time using my past as an excuse of why I could never trust him. When the truth was, the only person I couldn't trust was me.

Needless to say after my boyfriend found out, he told me he could no longer be with someone he couldn't trust, and I was completely devastated. I had been cheated on before, but I had no idea how horrible it felt to be the person that caused this kind of pain. I cried for weeks on end and learned a whole new plethora of gospel songs I had never even heard before. I just wanted the pain to stop. And resting at the feet of Christ was the only way I knew how. I never felt so broken in my entire life. Constantly asking myself, how did I get here? Who was I? How could I even do something like this to someone I loved? It was months after that I realized the saying was true. Hurt people, really do hurt people.

I looked in the mirror and no longer recognized the woman that was standing before me, I had truly lost the woman I was created to be. I thought to myself if I had just walked away when God told me to, maybe I wouldn't have felt so lost, maybe I wouldn't have lost everything. If you

If you are in a relationship and have to choose between losing the person you love or losing yourself, always choose you!

are in a relationship and have to choose between losing the person you love or losing yourself, always choose you.

Uncovering the Hurt

In the midst of my storm, I tried to understand, how in the world did I get here? I reminded myself at that point that to know where we are going, we have to know where we came from. I had to realize that my insecurities started long before my high school sweetheart cheated on me. They began as a little girl who never quite felt accepted or loved. We often wonder why a girl settles for less than she deserves. The reason I settled for less is because as a little girl I never dealt with the rejection I felt when a school boy crush never liked me back. I was so excited to finally have someone return my affection that I was too blind to see what was right in front of me. My first boyfriend didn't know how to value me; he didn't understand my worth, but how could he? When I didn't understand it for myself...

If you don't recognize your worth before you enter your first relationship, that relationship will define your worth for you. When parents shy away from asking or even thinking that their 8 or 9-year-old might be interested in someone, they are missing the opportunity to teach them that no matter how much a person is interested in you or not interested in you, it will never change the fact that you are special. I didn't know I was special and even worse I didn't know that not knowing that I was special was hurting the pieces of me that I was getting ready to give away.

I began to give away so much of myself in my previous relationships that I had no idea that I was building up so much anger and resentment every time a relationship didn't turn out the way I expected. I didn't know I could fuel so much anger, anger that was bottled up until I released my pain onto my unassuming boyfriend. However, how could I not have this much anger when in reality I never took the time to heal from the pain of my past?

The sad thing is I didn't even know that I hadn't forgive my previous boyfriends. I genuinely thought I had. It wasn't until I started to take the time for myself, to grow, that I realized the root of my pain. I heard a preacher talk about letting go of past relationships and at that moment I realized I hadn't fully let go. I didn't heal or forgive them for the things they had done in my past. I was carrying all that pain and baggage that I had ever felt into every other relationship. These issues were the kind of pain that influenced my behavior and caused me to ruin the fate of my future relationships. I had to learn how to heal.

I genuinely thought I was over the pain from my previous boyfriends because I never wanted any of them back, but I didn't truly forgive them or myself for what happened because I didn't learn from the pain. I didn't allow the lessons to make me better; I allowed them to make me bitter! I allowed it to make me insecure, impatient, needy and selfish.

So to heal and find freedom, I had to release the pain that held me back for so many years. The pain that kept me paralyzed, scared and unable to give my all to a relationship. This hurt paralyzed my ability to trust and led me to believe that I should always expect the worst from every man that I dated and that way I would never be disappointed. I was broken and didn't even know it.

All of those years I thought that I was in love, when in reality I was in love with the idea of 'love', the idea of being married and the idea that there was someone who wanted me as their wife. Not asking, are we compatible; are you the person God has specifically designed for me? When I sat down and asked myself did I evaluate my relationships in this way, the answer was NO!

I eventually realized that I wanted an idea, and marriage isn't just an idea. It's a union with the person God has designed for you, the person God specifically chose for you to fulfill his purpose with. It is a union where you will have to die daily to your own selfish and carnal desires. Of course I currently no longer want an idea, but back then I did. I didn't realize at the moment I was in love with love. So when my previous relationships didn't end in marriage, I was devastated, constantly asking God why you didn't answer my prayer. How could God answer my prayer, when God doesn't bless a mess!

God showed me when we step out of His will for our lives we go through consequences. I always wanted it my way in relationships. I knew how to get to married, you can step back, God. I got this. No, God, I can have sex with my boyfriend, this is going to be my husband. God had proven His authority over my life so many times. He must have gotten tired wondering how many times He had to teach me the same lesson. God showed me when you put anyone before Him, He will snatch them out of your life like a bad habit. He will rip them right out of it.

God doesn't care how much the rip hurts, because that same pain He uses to release you from your idols, is the same pain He will use to launch you into who He called you to be.

Forgiveness

To give my pain over to God, I had to learn about the gift of forgiveness. I never knew how much harboring unforgiveness in my heart could affect how I related to others. Holding on to unforgiveness influenced my behavior in my future relationships. I chose to act a certain way in my relationships so I wouldn't get hurt. I was bulletproof. No one could hurt me by cheating or deciding one day they wanted to leave me. If I acted a certain way or did certain things, I would ensure I wouldn't get hurt this time around. But, I was wrong. This kind of thinking was a total misconception on my behalf. All of the insecurities, impatience, selfishness and twisted mindset that I gained or held onto from previous painful relationships are what I realized contributed to the spiral that led me to hurt someone else. The pain I caused after cheating on my boyfriend showed me how tired I was of doing things my way; I had to learn to do it God's way.

To start fresh, one of the things I had to do was release my pride and tell all my ex-boyfriends that hurt me that I truly did forgive them. The resentment was not worth any more future relationships or the stunt in the spiritual level that God wanted to carry me to.

After learning how to forgive my previous boyfriends, I realized just how hard it was to sit on the other end of unforgiveness of someone else. No matter how many times I apologized to my ex-boyfriend who I hurt and tried to show him that I wasn't really like that, it didn't matter. I don't believe he ever quite looked at me the same again.

When you are the one waiting for forgiveness, there is always this smug idea that even if you miss what you had, at least it wasn't your fault that it fell apart. You can still sleep at night. When you are the one to blame for all of the hurt, you have to deal with the pain of missing that person, as well as the pain that comes along with knowing everything fell apart because of you.

When you care deeply for someone, watching them look at you with disappointment and disdain hurts the very core of who you are. I not only had to learn to wait for the forgiveness of others, but I also took a long time simply trying to forgive myself. When you mess up, you have to realize that you may never receive that source of relief that someone gives when they can truly forgive you for everything that you have put them through. However, if you continue to hold on to the pain from their unforgiveness, you will never truly be able to forgive yourself.

In life, we constantly make mistakes, but just because you make a mistake it doesn't mean you have to live there. You have to remember that no matter how many times you mess up, you are still a character worth rooting for. You are not your mistake, so don't you dare begin to live there.

Embracing the Hurt

The first step to healing the hurt you may have caused yourself or others can only happen when you recognize that you do have a problem. When I began to ask myself how I could ever be capable of cheating on someone like I did, I had to be honest with myself and realize that these traits didn't happen overnight. These traits were a result of years and years of pain that I continued to foster in my heart against others and instead of dealing with the pain, I suppressed it.

One of the reasons we suppress the pain from a previous relationship instead of dealing with it is because a lot of us do not like to be alone. Whenever the pastor quotes the Scripture "two is better than one", we want to rush and raise our hands in agreement because we are utterly fearful of being alone. When you are alone, you don't have someone to go on dates with or someone to remind you how special you are. When you are not alone, you feel less fearful of winding up like that older single woman or man in your church that never got the chance to get married. Our fear of being alone is greater than the fear we have that we may destroy our God-given destiny, by refusing to be alone long enough to deal with our toxic situations.

When we make the choice to be alone with ourselves and our thoughts, we have the opportunity to evaluate who we are, the good, the bad and the ugly. Relationships are purposeful when we enter them with a full understanding of who God created us to be and our true purpose in life. When we don't enter into a relationship with this understanding, we use our new found interest as a distraction from the process needed to understand ourselves. We get so excited about getting to know someone else but ignore the opportunities to get to know our self.

Most people would believe that it goes without saying, of course, I love me. However, if we do love ourselves, how is it that we shy away from spending time alone? Why do we run from painful situations instead of truly evaluating how they have affected us? Why do we settle to date "good for right now" instead of patiently waiting for "God's best"? Don't we feel we deserve God's best?

I didn't realize that I didn't love me. I didn't love me enough to wait on God's best. I didn't love me enough to heal from my previous pain and I didn't love me enough not to hurt someone else, as well as myself during the process. The acceptance of my need for spiritual growth taught me that my situation would never change unless I faced the reality of the rejection, hurt and insecurities within me. If I wanted God to change who I used to be, into whom he created me to be, I had to heal the hurt by facing the truth. God told me that "Everything you are going through is preparing you for everything that you asked for. There are blogs, books, sermons, workshops, mentorship and motivational speeches just waiting to be birthed inside of you. I'm just waiting for you…"

Growth Exercise:

1. Evaluate and pray about any hurt that you still haven't dealt with from your past.

2. Forgive and release any pain or mistrust that you are holding onto from your previous relationships.

3. Apologize and seek forgiveness from anyone you may have hurt in the past.

Chapter 4

The Common Denominator Is You

As a 27-year-old, I took a look back at previous romantic relationships and realized I failed at every one of them. So I decided to ask God why? If you are bold enough also to ask this question, I caution you to prepare yourself for Christ's response. You see when you give God permission to wreck you, to show you the dark areas of your life you have to be ready for him to reveal some painful realities. If you are constantly asking yourself why you keep dating guys or girls that never seem to be worth it. If you regret every single ex you have ever dated, then the problem may not be your ex. The problem may just be you. So instead of playing the blame game, take a minute to evaluate you. Pat Bailey once said, "We are not nearly as right as we think we are, and others are not nearly as wrong as we like to believe." I sincerely believe that you are what you attract.

A few years ago I was completely broken and at that time I didn't realize it: dysfunction attracts dysfunction. You can't attract a mate who is whole or understands their purpose if you

> You can't attract a mate who is whole or understands their purpose if you haven't done the same.

haven't done the same. Amos 3:3 (NIV) says, "How can two walk together unless they agree?" The more time we spend running away from the truth of who we are, the longer we will remain chained to the brokenness of our past.

At some point, you have to realize that although your exes may have some blame to share in your failed relationships, the bigger picture clearly shows that the common denominator in every one of your previous failed relationships is you. The one common factor is that they all involved you, and the only person you can change is you! Doing the same thing over and over and expecting different results is the definition of insanity. If you want something you never had before, even if that thing is peace in your season of singleness, you have to be willing to do something you've never done. We can't expect to have the relationships we always wanted if we are continually reflecting the person that we don't want. During my one year challenge, I had to learn to evaluate myself and the characteristics I was possibly displaying. In that process I discovered insecurity, low self-esteem, selfishness, impatience, loneliness, attention-seeking and self-absorbed, arrogance, pride and lust.

Insecurity

The most painful thing about insecurities is that most people have no clue they are insecure. It's because we often think that insecure people are only people who walk around with shrugged shoulders and their head held down. However just because I don't walk around with my head hung low, doesn't mean I don't feel inadequate inside. Merriam-Webster's definition of insecure reads:

"deficient in assurance: beset by fear and anxiety." Most insecure people have this underlying fear that they are fighting with but may not be verbally sharing with their partner. But if you look closely, we are expressing it in our demeanor. Have you ever heard the expression "actions speak louder than words"? I have listed 10 actions below that reveal insecurity.

1. You are always nervous to tell your significant other how you feel.

2. You are constantly accusing your partner of cheating or thinking about cheating on you.

3. You are afraid your partner will leave you one day.

4. You are extremely jealous, (social media stalking, going through private phone messages, and constantly questioning them of their whereabouts).

5. You need to spend every waking moment with them, and you forbid them to have relationships with certain people.

6. You are depressed if you are not in a relationship.

7. You prefer to stay in an unhealthy relationship rather than to be alone.

8. You make excuses for your partner's dysfunctional behaviors.

9. You don't trust your partner to tell you the truth.

10. You don't trust God to bring you a relationship that reflects His love or your worth.

If you can find yourself saying yes to one or more of the things on this list, then chances are you struggle with insecurity. All of these actions are driven by fear and anxiety. Fear tells you are not good enough for your significant other, and that's why they will cheat or leave. Fear also makes us believe that we are not good enough for God to bless us with a purposeful relationship and that's why we stay.

Therefore, we sometimes put up with dysfunction or use unhealthy vices to 'protect' our relationship because we don't want to end up alone. However, if God has ordained your relationship, and you have placed God in the driver's seat, there is no reason to have fear or anxiety about it not working out. We are insecure because we don't want God to decide, we want what we think is best.

I wouldn't describe myself as someone that ever walked around with their shoulders down or head hung low. I am an extrovert in every sense of the word. I am extremely social, and if you ever met me you would think that I was one of the most confident people in the world. However with all that 'confidence', I can honestly say I remember a time when I engaged in almost every single thing on this list above: the social media stalking, the constant questioning and the constant fear of losing my relationship and ending up alone. These fears controlled my mind and my actions, and at the time I had no idea that I was completely insecure. Your relationship is like a ball of sand in your hands. If you hold it too tightly, eventually every grain of it will slip away.

If you feel this list doesn't apply to you but is just like every person you have ever dated. Please don't think you're exempt from this list, *Insecurity breeds insecurity*. So if you are wondering why you keep ending up with someone who does these things, take a look in the mirror. Your insecurity may manifest itself in a different way, but it's still insecurity. You will attract and stay with someone who displays these habits because you are not secure enough to know that you deserve better.

Every day there is a constant battle to prove that you are ok with God's timing. However, your insecurity keeps telling you to take your relationships into your hands. I won't sit here and tell you it's easy. For some of us we have to literally get up every single morning and fight. Ephesians 6:12 (NIV) says, "we don't wrestle against flesh and blood, but we wrestle against spiritual warfare in high places." So I had to learn to pray. You have to pray and make the choice to say God, I give my will over to you. I prayed for peace, and I continue to commit to releasing the fear and anxiety that has constantly held me back, over to God!

Low Self-Esteem

People who have low self-esteem sing a "woe is me" song. As I mentioned, I was never the girl that got the guy growing up. My acne during my teenage years was horrific. So there were days where I didn't feel pretty or confident. When you grow up not valuing the amazing things about you, you sometimes settle for someone that may not even deserve you. If you can't sit down and write a list of 20 things that you love about yourself internally and externally, then you may be suffering from low self-esteem. If you can't recognize all the amazing things about you, how can you expect anyone else to?

I think if we're honest at some point, we all go through a moment where we believe, "Well, I may be special, but I don't think I'm good enough for that person." They're too smart, too good looking, too rich, too driven or too religious for them to notice me. Then what happens if they do notice you, but you realize they're not everything you thought they would be? When you have low self-esteem, you still stay because he is good looking and has a great job. It's ok that he flirts with other women because it's better than being alone. For men, maybe she has a banging body and makes a whole lot of money. So you think, it's ok that she verbally abuses me, because once again it's better than being alone. These excuses are simply tools of the enemy that help to feed your low self-esteem.

In dating, you shouldn't be picky by getting caught up in an extremely long shallow checklist. However, you can't forget your worth either. Everyone should have at least three to five non-negotiable traits. Traits you know you're worth having in a mate. My non-negotiables are:

1. He has to love God more than He loves me, obedient and fully engaged in a relationship with Christ.

2. He has to understand his purpose and I have to have clearance from God on how our purposes will align.

3. I want to have an attraction to his mind, body, and soul. I want to have a genuine connection and chemistry with my husband; I want him to be my earthly best friend.

If you have never made a list of your non-negotiable traits, I also challenge you to pray about those and give those over to God. You deserve a partner that will love and value you. So stop believing you are not pretty enough, smart enough, or 'saved' enough to marry God's best for you. If you feel you do value yourself but have dated others who have not, then you have to realize you still have some searching to do because you cling to what you represent. You either know your worth, or you settle for someone who believes they are beneath you because you are too afraid to be rejected by someone who does know who they are. So don't take the long way around the track to realize that if you are dating someone with low self-esteem, it means you may have a low self-esteem too!

Low self-esteem is just another way of telling God, "God, You messed up, and I don't believe that You made me good enough." Genesis 1:27 (NIV) tells us that "Christ created us in his image." If you believe the image of God is special, then remember, so are you. So if you have suffered from low self-esteem, I want to remind you that you are good enough and that you are perfect for the heart that was made to love you.

Selfishness

If anyone has ever called you selfish, whether it was your significant other, mother, brother or friend you should evaluate their words before you get married. If you are married, you should evaluate these words before your marriage gets any worse. Often, like insecurity, a lot of people don't realize they are selfish. Often leaving the people who bear the brunt of your selfishness confused to why you can't possibly see it. Coming from a person who has often displayed many selfish traits, it's important to know that people show their selfishness in different ways.

My Way is the Right Way.

The reason people believe they are not selfish is because they tend only to remember that they have allowed others to have their way before. I once had an argument with a guy I was working with on a project, and I told him "You always want us to do things your way." He shouted back that it was simply not true. He then sought to give me a long list of things we did that came out of suggestions I made. I said that's not being unselfish because the only time my suggestions were valued was when he didn't have a suggestion at all or he simply had no interest in what was being decided. An unselfish person is willing to listen actively and seek to understand another person's suggestion even when the suggestion is in polarizing opposition to what they want to do.

My Needs are More Important than Yours.

People who are selfish don't realize that sacrificing their needs and desires so that the other person can be happy is all a part of a healthy relationship.

I remember I was once dating a guy and after church on New Year's Eve, I wanted to go to this party. So I said to him, "Do you want to go to this party or somewhere else?" He told me he would just prefer to go home and get some rest. I then replied, "No problem, we will just go to this party, but we won't stay too long, so you can go home and rest?" That's a great compromise right? Wrong! Did I have to go to that party? No, but when you are selfish you are blind to the other person's needs. He was sick, and I was still trying to get my party in because that's what was important to me. That was selfish. I didn't realize at the time, but it was.

This same guy once picked me up for church one Sunday, he was late and when I got in the car, I saw an empty Burger King bag and a half eaten breakfast sandwich on the seat. I was furious, we were already late, and he stopped to get breakfast and even worse he didn't even bring any for me, and I'm selfish? I thought to myself. However at that moment the Holy Spirit told me to be silent. So once we began driving he told me the half of sandwich that was sitting there was for me. He went on to explain that on his way out the house, his dad had brought him breakfast so he ate half and left the other half there for me because he figured I would've been hungry. I wanted to melt; I was the selfish one. If you are in a relationship, especially a marriage, your first thought should always be how I can serve you, not how can I be served.

Manipulation

These people are often intellectuals. They don't blatantly tell you they want things to go their way. They use mind games to get you to do what they want you to do. They often play the victim role by crying or telling you a sad story to get you to see things their way. "I just wanted a diamond ring because growing up my parents refused to ever buy me anything, but they always got my sister what she wanted. I just want someone who loves me to show me they care." Without even knowing it, you are hooked.

People who are manipulative are dangerous because they are not only forcing you to do things their way; they also want to keep you blind to the process. Therefore, a manipulative person is not looking for a partner; they are looking for someone they can control. A controlling spirit is a selfish spirit. As a stubborn person,

I often wanted things to go my way. I did it so much I didn't even realize when I was using the power of manipulation. That's the sad thing about negative traits; the enemy keeps us blind to the fact that we are using them.

If you have been in a relationship where you have broken up multiple times after your partner was angry about the way you treated them. Every time you go back, they are conditioning you to what punishment looks and feels like when you don't do what they say, that is manipulation. The minute you agree to go back to the dysfunction, they know that they are in control and will continue to train you to give them what they want. God is not a God of confusion. If there is a disagreement as a couple, you should use communication to get through it, not manipulation. Your desire to serve or please your mate should be because you want to love and respect them as Christ does the Church. You should never have to use manipulation to teach someone how to love you, and you should also never have to be the victim of manipulation to love or serve your partner.

Self-absorbed / Attention Seekers

Someone who is an attention seeker gets an extreme high from other people complimenting or stroking their ego. We all like to hear nice things, but when we do these things in the sacrifice of who they may hurt in the process, that is a result of being self-absorbed. Self-absorbed, older, married men tend to flirt with younger girls because they want to make sure they "still got it". Selfish women who are married or have been in a relationship for a long time may not have heard sweet nothings from their partner in awhile.

As an attention seeker, I used to be filled with butterflies when an attractive admirer or ex-boyfriend told me how undeniably beautiful I was. When you place value on receiving attention over authentic love, you create a slippery slope.

There were so many times I asked myself, wouldn't it have been easier to simply say to my partner "my love tank is empty"? I used to be so afraid to communicate this, that in the end, lack of communication caused so much unnecessary pain. You may think that to say to your partner, "I've never cheated on you, but sometimes I feel like I want to cheat because my love tank is empty," it will cause strife, but imagine how much pain you will cause if you cheated. A non-selfish person recognizes a problem and communicates maturely with their partner.

Believe me when I say causing pain to your partner by emotionally cheating is heartbreaking. Attention seekers must realize that they will never really fill that void through various empty compliments. Christ is the only one who can fill your emptiness. When we realize that the desire to be whole is a yearning for Christ, we will stop putting unrealistic expectations on our partner.

If you are not selfish, then you may be wondering "Well, I'm not selfish, how is it that I keep ending up with people who are?" Well, it's both because you suffer from insecurity or low self-esteem, and you feel this is the best you can do. You say to yourself, "No one is perfect and dealing with their selfishness is better than starting over." You may even be arrogant and believe one day you can change them. As I once heard someone say, the only time you can change a man or woman is when they are in diapers. You have to give that person over to God and pray that He would one day help them recognize and change their selfish behavior on their own.

Arrogant and Prideful

Most people will never admit to being arrogant or prideful. However just like insecurities, arrogance or pride can tend to reside within our actions without us knowing it. I often call arrogant people overconfident insecure individuals. Throughout dating, I have encountered three types of arrogant behavior.

The Overconfident Enabler

This person loves to date people who have low self-esteem or are insecure. Often an arrogant person may only feel secure in a relationship where the person shows them that they can't live without them. The dysfunction of needing someone to make you feel loved is like a drug. They may argue when their significant other displays extremely jealous behavior or forbids them to speak to someone; however they will never really leave. And often their willingness to stay makes loved ones wonder why their friend may stick around to go through it all over again. Well, part of the reason is that whether they care to admit it or not they feed off of their partner's negative energy, 'love' and drama. Some people will say, "If they don't act crazy about me or make me feel like I make up their entire world then they must not love me."

They often believe they are so special that they have to be with someone who adores them and puts them on a pedestal to feel loved. Someone who is willing to fight for or over them makes them feel secure. When in reality, the majority of the time they are just too insecure to be in a healthy relationship. Arrogant people fear a partner who is not obsessed with them because it means that one day that person may leave. The obsession has become normal to them, and anything not on that level makes them feel as if the person is not genuinely interested. I was a good fit for someone with this need because my insecurities and low self-esteem would feed the ego of those that need affirmation. It's true that you attract what you reflect.

The Savior

This applies to anyone who believes they can 'save' someone from a toxic situation or themselves. In two of my 'significant' relationships, I thought that I was doing the right thing by being a 'savior'. However, I was completely misled because Christ is the only one who can save. My insecurity of wanting to be wanted and adored were fuel by the statements that "you are better than the person I am currently with." I loved hearing "you are such a good woman," "You are the ONLY good that can "save" me from this toxic relationship." I was arrogant, and an arrogant person feeds off a person telling them how much better you are at listening and understanding me than my current partner is, or my ex was. Not realizing that one day, I too would be the ex with various shortcomings that they would be telling someone new about in future times to come.

Instead of running from these situations, my arrogant counselor role kicked in. It would often be because a relationship was on the rocks, and I would tell them how they desperately needed to leave. The fact that they were still in the situation when I met them should have told me they were already too insecure to leave on their own. I was the emotional 'other woman' until they left that woman for me.

When you are secure, no matter how much you think someone needs to be 'saved', you wouldn't be attracted to their brokenness. Pain shouldn't bond you, trust issues shouldn't be the thing you have in common, your wholeness should be your link. However when you lack a certain level of self-awareness, you don't even realize that you are making this kind of decision.

The Unforgiver

This person is filled with pride because in their eyes, they have never done anything wrong. I remember this one guy I was "dating", who was furious with his ex-girlfriend for something she did with her current boyfriend. At that moment, I realized two things. First, he was clearly not over her because why was this even an issue? Second, we can often be judgmental and self-righteous when we believe that the other person has done more dirt than us. You see he had broken up with this girl because she had cheated on him, so anything else she did just added to the pile of her 'unrighteousness'. After he kept insisting that she had reached an all-time low, he said he didn't even know who she was anymore. I asked him how he could be so judgmental? None of them had professed to be Christians, so I didn't even understand by which moral code he was choosing to judge her. He ignored my plea. My caution to all of us is to remember that we all have sinned and come short of the glory of God.

People mess up and just because they made a mistake, it doesn't mean every other thing they do in life is crippled. People are killing relationships because they stayed and refused to forgive or left and still refused to forgive. Maybe you never cheated and yes, my situation taught me to empathize more with people who have made this mistake, but we should all learn to be less prideful because we all sin. Unforgiveness says that I'm too prideful to see the good in you, because I know I would have never made that mistake. We can't afford to hold someone up to a 'judgmental chart' for the rest of their life because we all make mistakes, and Christ forgives us every day for those mistakes. I often tell people, don't judge me just because I may sin differently than you.

Lustful Desires

A few months ago, I began to pride myself on being celibate for almost three years until I watched a sermon that wrecked me. The sermon talked about being celibate in the physical but still being impure in the mind. This sermon taught me that even though being celibate is a good thing we must remember not to pride

> When you give your body, mind, heart or soul to someone that God didn't design for you, you are hurting Christ and yourself.

ourselves on our ability to be celibate, we should strive for purity in every sense of the word. When you are over confident about the practice of celibacy, you have to ask yourself, are you doing this for Christ or self-praise? As a single person, you should choose a life of purity because of your love for God. When you give your body, mind, heart or soul to someone that God didn't design for you, you are hurting Christ and yourself. That attachment whether you, believe it or not, is killing all the beautiful things He has placed in you.

I remember one of the greatest lessons I heard on purity. The speaker wanted to inform the young ladies in the room that purity is more than abstinence from the physical act of sex. Purity consists of your emotional, spiritual, mental and physical self. Imagine that each component represents a leg of a chair or table. As you compromise any portion of these areas, your ability to stay pure becomes weaker. The same way the stability of a chair or table would be compromised if any of its legs were removed.

Spiritual Purity

Spiritual purity is compromised when you don't pay attention to what you feed your spirit through movies, music, and even books. I always told one of my friends that I hated reading romantic novels. So needless to say unlike every other avid reader, *Fifty Shades of Grey* was not on my must read list. Those books filled with erotic and sexual emotions filled my spirit with yearnings and thoughts that were already hard to deal with as a single, celibate woman. When we feed our spirits with these thoughts and images, these images and thoughts eventually become our images and desires.

Mental Purity

Mental purity consists of your thoughts. When you say, I can think about sex as long as I'm not doing it right? You are only fooling yourself. Thinking I can have phone sex or continually visualize what I would like to do with my significant other because I don't ever intend on doing anything physical is a slippery slope. I've made this mistake before. I knew the person was in a relationship but never once told them or told anyone else that I found this person attractive. I would visualize them and got excited about their physical appearance every time I saw them. I didn't see it as a bad thing because I would never act on those thoughts. I thought everything was fine too, until one day it wasn't. The person gave me a ride to my car and we engaged in a quick ten minute innocent conversation.

Shockingly enough I was texted later that day with them expressing their attraction towards me and that they felt my energy towards them from the day they met me. WHAT??? We had met six months before this conversation happened. I didn't realize I was giving off signs of flirtation; I thought I was so discreet. Embarrassed, I had no clue my mental impurity was being transferred to my actions. I eventually cut off the mentally impure thoughts as well as the friendship. I didn't want to compromise other areas of my purity, or place myself in a compromising position. Proverbs 4:23 (NIV) "Above all else guard your heart, from everything you do, flows from it."

Emotional Purity

Emotional purity is compromised when we begin to allow our love for someone to develop to such an intense level that we wish to give ourselves to that person. When our words become promises and vows without the commitment of marriage it is scary. As a single person making intense emotional promises and connections can be damaging because if the relationship doesn't last you have already established an emotional soul tie. When you give away an intense emotional component of yourself, you are compromising your ability to remain sober and emotionally pure. In the Pinterest Love story where Amanda Roman and Ryan Leak were engaged and married on the same day, after five years of dating, neither of them had ever said the words "I love you" to each other. They both explained they didn't want to say words that were so intense unless they were able to back it up with a lifetime commitment. I'm not saying if you tell your girlfriend or boyfriend I love you that you are emotionally impure. Their story just served as a reminder to me that there are ways to guard your heart on your road to courtship and if you are super emotional like me, placing your emotions at the feet of Christ is a good thing.

Physical Impurity

Physical impurity is any form of sexual intercourse. We often push the limits in this area and still believe that we are pure in the eyes of God. However, if you are on the fence on your physical purity, a good practice involves setting boundaries. Once you have crossed a line in this area, it's hard for you to remain pure. Therefore, I had to learn to give myself boundaries. I encourage avoiding the caress or touching of private areas. Pray about your choices and the boundaries you set. It takes a lot of strength to present yourself physically pure before God, but it's not impossible.

If you have lustful thoughts, you will still attract those who have a lustful spirit. I remember asking myself, as a celibate woman, why was I still attracting men who thought that it was ok to have a sexual relationship with me? I had to evaluate what pictures I put on social media. What energy was I giving off in the things I said, watched or even found funny? If someone can tell by your actions and demeanor, that sex before marriage is off the table, if that is what they are interested in, most won't even approach you. However for the bold ones that still do, your presence alone should quickly make them understand that you are serious about practicing what you preach. You have to set boundaries up for yourself and demand that those boundaries be respected. I had to make a conscious decision that I no longer wanted just to be celibate. I wanted to present myself emotionally, mentally, spiritually and physically pure before God. I believe if you don't establish this level of purity eventually, there will be a high chance that the inevitable will happen, and your table will collapse.

So if you have evaluated your levels of insecurity, low self-esteem, selfishness, arrogance, and lust and found that one or more of these do apply to you, then I strongly urge you to take some time to work on you. Stop asking God why can't I find someone who will settle down? Why can't I find a faithful partner? Why can't he or she be straight with me? The thing is God can't send this kind of man or woman because you are not ready. God can't fix your marriage because you refuse to deal with your personal issues. If you struggle with any of these common denominators, God is trying to get your attention to transform you into the person he has called you to be.

When you crave attention from a significant other, it's because your value is coming from their words and not from Christ. Stop asking God to get on board with your timeline and get on board with His. Marcel Proust once said, "True discovery consists not in finding new landscapes but in seeing the same landscapes with new eyes." You are a beautiful masterpiece created by God, and He's just waiting for you to see it. You deserve a God fearing relationship, but you can't keep approaching relationships the same way you did before.

The past and the way you did things before may be comfortable, and the future can be scary, but God is challenging you to become comfortable with the unknown. If you don't have the proper foundation, your future relationships will be ruined. Social media, friends, and some older persons base your worth on if you have a mate. Don't allow these pressures to define you, because when you allow a relationship to define you, you will stay in toxic situations for the sake of the relationship. Whether you see the relationship as healthy or not, it doesn't matter, it should never define who you are as a person.

Falling in love with you first, is the best gift that you can give yourself. The only way to fall in love with you is by turning to the one who created you. Christ is willing and able to heal you from all of the dysfunctional traits that you have nurtured over the years. I had to take the time to allow myself to develop into everything on that list of qualities that I hope to one day attract in a mate. Although the journey has been a long one, I never once regretted taking the step to begin doing love, God's way.

Growth Exercise:

1. Be honest and evaluate any personal issues that you have that may have contributed to the downfall of your previous relationships?

2. Write down ways that you can overcome any selfishness, insecurity, low self-esteem, impatience, loneliness, attention-seeking/self-absorbed, arrogant/prideful and lustful behaviors that may still be a struggle for you.

MEDITATION

Chapter 5

Accepting the Challenge

At the beginning of 2013, I decided to take Andy Stanley's one year challenge. The One Year Challenge dares singles that have been dating their way and making selfish decisions throughout their previous relationships to take a YEAR off from dating. The purpose of the one year challenge is for singles to learn how to love God, love themselves and to eventually learn how to date God's way. At the beginning of December, (the month before) during a low moment in my life, I asked a spiritual mentor, how did he know his wife was the 'one'? He said to me, everything he was looking for, he found in her. When I looked at him for elaboration, he said, "Instead of elaborating, I just want you to watch something." It was the series *The New Rules of Love Sex and Dating*.

Excited about this new sound advice, I rushed home to watch it that same day. However, when I got to Sermon #2 and heard the one year challenge issued, I shut that computer DOWN like a bad habit! "Take a year off Lord", I said, "God are you serious? I'm 27, ain't nobody got time for that!" You see I was in a relationship that was on the brink of working, in my eyes at least. My then ex-boyfriend and I were about to get back together, I could feel it! However my plans didn't pan out how I expected. My feelings were wrong, and God didn't work it out MY way. Woody Allen was so right when he said; "You want to make God laugh, simply tell him your plans." So needless to say, God's plans were not my plans, and so I had to move on.

So during January 2013, after fasting for a long time and beginning to read the *Purpose Driven Life*, I knew I had to make some changes and trust God to take over my love life. So January 30th, 2013 I made a commitment not to date unless I felt God wanted me to be with that person. A little over a month later in early March I saw someone advertising Andy Stanley's series on Facebook. I had blocked it out so much that I only recognized the title *The New Rules of Love, Sex, and Dating*.

Was I the person, the person I was looking for, was looking for?

I remembered then that I started to watch it but didn't finish the series. I didn't remember anything else about it or the reason I didn't finish it. So I pulled it up once again, heard the one year challenge issued and instantly remembered why I didn't want to hear this crap. But this time I listened to all of it and then said "Alright, alright Lord I get it, I am going to be obedient and take a year off from dating geez! Jan 30th, 2014, I will resume dating." Sigh! It wasn't easy, but I knew it would be worth it. Taking a year off took a lot of self-control but it proved to be such a WORTHWHILE and rewarding experience. It challenged me to ask myself the focal point of the series "Was I the person, the person I was looking for, was looking for?"

Proverbs 8:35 (NIV) says, "Whoever finds the Lord, finds life, and receives favor from the Lord." Christ wanted me to get empty for him. He wanted me to press into my calling and boldly step into the plans that He had for me and if you're reading this book, I truly believe He wants to do the same for you.

Andy Stanley had been giving the advice to take the year challenge for over twenty years. However, he admitted that very few single people often took his advice out of the lack of motivation to begin to prepare for a marriage that they could not see. For those singles who took the advice, he boasted that they usually all came back to him as a newlywed. These men and women thanked him for the encouragement to focus on becoming the one, instead of obsessing about finding the 'one'. This advice had proved to be an amazing catalyst to the healthy marriages that they all were currently experiencing. This marriage was the kind of marriage that I wanted.

Now listen to me carefully, I'm not saying that the person will be there immediately after you take this one year commitment. I am telling you that whenever God blesses you with a spouse you will be more prepared for that relationship than ever before. I truly believe that the road to becoming the person you are looking for is priceless and if you have never been married before you get the opportunity to get marriage right the first time!

Andy eloquently shared that promises are no substitute for preparation. Preparation makes you capable; a promise makes you accountable. Promises mean nothing if you haven't been prepared to fulfill them. You can't fail to study for a test and then expect to pass. You have to prepare adequately. There are thousands of unhappily married people who failed to prepare for a commitment and are living in a painful promise that they never knew how to keep.

Andy cautions that unfortunately it's usually married people who hear this message and understand the urgency of this preparation. Married men and women understand that they are currently going through rough patches in their marriage because they didn't take the time they never knew they needed, to prepare to become the right person. When you spend time becoming the 'one', your development during this process forces you to choose someone whose lifestyle will coincide with yours.

I had to learn the hard way that God won't give you what you desire until He feels you are ready for it. When I think about that statement I remember a saying I once heard, "There are marriages men put together and ones that God put together." I don't know about you, but I want to enter a marriage that Christ has put together. I want to enjoy my union as a whole person with the whole person God designed for me. So I had to take a look in the mirror and ask myself, was I ready to get on the road to becoming a whole and healthy person?

Some of the topics in this series that really resonated with me focused on addressing unresolved childhood issues by forming a better relationship with your parents, renewing your mind by breaking bad habits, getting out of debt, becoming financially stable and also getting involved in your local church.

Address your Unresolved Childhood Issues

If you want to figure out where you might have gone wrong, start at the beginning. Seek to address any potential unresolved childhood issues. The first relationship we experience is with our parents. Whether we care to recognize it or not, this relationship plays a big role in how we will relate to others going forward. To help you break down a little better where you may fall with your parents, I want to share the message the Holy Spirit gave to me of four possible parent/child relationships.

Physically & Emotionally Present:

I believe that this is the best chance for children to have a great opportunity of being in a relationship that is not strained by 'mommy and daddy issues'. When a child spends quality time with their parents, while also emotionally connecting with them, they will tend to have a healthy view of what a great relationship looks like. A great example of a parent that is emotionally and physically present, I saw this YouTube video of the father who dressed up to take his little girl on her very first date. He wanted to teach his daughter that she was truly special. He wanted her to see how she should be treated and respected. He set the pace and therefore, any man who approached her in the future would have to live up to the standard set by her dad.

I think it's also important to note that you can be a child of divorce or unwed parents and still have both parents who are physically and emotionally present in your life. My mother grew up with unwed parents who were both actively present in her life. I urge parents to realize how fundamental it is to nurture this relationship at an early age with their children whether or not they are still together. Co-parenting is the mature way to ensure the success of your child.

Physically Present / Emotionally Absent:

I think this is a category that a lot of old school parents may experience. I simply believe they are ignorant of the fact that they're not giving their child everything they need. Growing up, providing a good life for your child was the only request. How could their child have issues, when they as a parent have been physically present at every important juncture of their child's life? What parents must realize is that emotional connection still plays a vital role in determining your child's self-worth.

In-depth conversations with my dad always felt random and awkward, so I never had them or sought every opportunity to make them as short as possible. Therefore, I never established an emotional attachment with my dad. He was physically present in everything I did. However I couldn't say that he knew who I was as a person, he didn't know how things made me feel, and more importantly he didn't know how I felt about myself. My dad didn't grow up in a house where they constantly talked about their feelings, so he had no idea that he wasn't giving me everything that I needed. However not having my worth affirmed by my father led me to search for that affirmation and approval from other men.

Physically & Emotionally Unstable:

This involves parents who pop in now and then to physically and emotionally be there but then tend to disappear for long periods of time. This kind of in-and-out relationship forms trust issues. As a child, they develop insecurity that men or women are untrustworthy, and it will be a bad idea ever to become emotionally attached to someone. They expect the worst, while secretly still hoping for the best. I cried at the stories my best friend would tell me growing up, about her father who would promise to take her on a day out and never showed up. But, there were one or two memories where he had seemed to want to make a relationship work. If this was a part of your childhood reality, this unresolved issue could be one of the reasons it's been so hard for you to deal with some of your relationship problems.

Physically & Emotionally Absent:

Even if it's one parent who has been completely absent, it's a hard thing for a child to miss out on the experience of what a healthy relationship looks like (in any sense of the word). These children have never had a physical or emotional connection with their parent and sometimes have to fight to figure out how future relationships should look. A lot of times, children who have lost a parent to death fall into this category as well. In our society, therapy is frowned upon and therefore the majority of children are never exposed to grief counseling, leaving the child to deal with a myriad of suppressed emotions on their own. I've noticed that children who don't deal with the death of a parent a lot of times have a mixture of unresolved feelings. I believe that no matter what the reason is that a child is missing out on this experience, not addressing these issues can be detrimental to this child's future relationships.

Once you have identified which category you may fall in, if you've never taken the time to pray and ask God to reveal the life changing moments of your past for you, I encourage you to do so now. When I began the year challenge, I decided to begin weekly lunch dates with my dad. After explaining my concerns to him, we both wanted to make an effort to bond more on an emotional level. The first few times we had lunch were a bit awkward but eventually the conversations got easier. Our relationship is still a work in progress, but I was so glad that we got the opportunity to become a lot closer than we were before. If you still have the opportunity to mend a broken relationship with a parent or parents I would strongly suggest you use this time during this year to build on that relationship.

For those who may not have that opportunity because of an unwilling parent or death, I want to remind you to pray about that unwilling parent and also to remember that you also have a Heavenly Father that is crazy about you. I love the words to Anthony Brown's song that says, "You thought I was worth saving, so you came into my life. You thought I was worth keeping, so you filled me up inside. You thought I was to die for, so you sacrificed your life." No matter what your situation may be, God wants you to know you are truly special and worth it. Above all else let your relationships with your Heavenly Father fulfill your worth. Forgive your earthly parents and if they're not present, I strongly encourage you to seek a mentor or active family member to help continue to nurture you in the love of God.

Renew your Mind: Break your Bad Habits

In Chapter 3, we spoke in depth about the personal issues that we hold on to that make it hard for us to have a healthy relationship. It was important for me to use that year to work on those issues.

I had to learn patience because change doesn't happen overnight. I was 27 when I began the year challenge therefore that was 27 years of numerous bad traits that I had to correct. I had to bear in mind that this transformation wouldn't be a magical turn around; it would be a continual building process. It would take a while to release everything that held me back from having purposeful relationships: fear, anxiousness, insecurity, selfishness, a lack of trust and a lack of boundaries. Even though this journey of releasing bad habits would be hard, God showed me that trying to get rid of them during a marriage would be a lot harder.

God didn't allow me to take insecurity, pain, resentment and unforgiveness into a marriage. This brokenness would have been my foundation, and I thank God that He didn't allow it. I had to use this time to get hidden in the love of God. God had to mold me, shape me and transform me into the person He called me to be without all of the extra baggage. Honestly, at first I felt like I was too old to start the one year challenge, but God revealed to me, no matter where you are in life, it's never too late. If you are currently still struggling with your personal issues in your marriage, it is still never too late to give those issues back over to God and work on your marriage.

Get out of Debt: Financial Stability

In one of my favorite shows Girlfriends, the character Toni unknowingly married her husband Todd while he was $750,000 in debt. Although this was a fictional TV character, marrying someone with a huge amount of debt is still a reality for a lot of couples today. It would seem like something like this should have been talked about, however the euphoria of getting the chance to be married superseded this conversation. We should learn to have these hard discussions before it's too late. In future relationships, we have to be willing to ask, do you tithe? How do you spend your money? Do you save? Do you struggle with debt?

Andy encourages individuals to get out of debt on their own even before they even enter a courtship. He stressed the fact that an individual's debt will decrease a lot faster on their own rather than having the strain of reducing a combined debt while also trying to build a life together with your spouse. He explained that this time alone should also be geared to budgeting your individual finances.

Getting out of debt wasn't a big problem for me but remaining financially responsible and stable was. As a wedding planner, I watched so many brides panic at the actual cost of planning a wedding, along with all of the finances involved in building a life together after their 'big day'. Additionally, credit card bills, car notes and student loans combined with these upcoming events can provide an extra financial strain. It is important to avoid letting the reality of budgeting scare you once there is a ring on your finger.

Proverbs 14:8 (NIV) says, "The wisdom of the prudent is to give a thought to their ways, but the folly of fools is deception." If being financially responsible is something you struggle with, attending financial seminars or sitting down one-on-one with a financial advisor or mentor will help you to put your financial responsibilities in perspective. The best advice I ever received from a financial advisor was to make a list of my current amount of debt and my current amount of savings. After this, it was important to budget out my monthly salary with a goal to decrease my debt and increase my savings, while balancing my everyday responsibilities. I had to tell myself, "If you don't want a marriage with financial strain, I strongly suggest that you make a commitment to yourself to begin to make sound financial choices starting today!"

Get Involved in your Local Church

Making the decision to begin the one year challenge forced me to cut off certain flirtatious relationships as well as certain friendships leaving a lot of idol time for my mind to wander and miss my old lifestyle. At first, my commitment to my church helped to serve as a distraction from my previous life. But, I soon realized that serving Christ eventually helped me to develop my abilities and talents. By getting involved in my local church and other positive activities, I learned just how much I enjoyed hosting, motivational speaking, writing, and event planning. Getting involved in your local church will help you to discover and use those God-given gifts.

In fact, six months into my year challenge I felt strong that this was a message that I wanted every single young person to hear. I approached my spiritual mentor that introduced me to the series and asked him to partner with me in hosting a four week *New Rules of Love Sex and Dating* conference. I had never done anything like this before. However, I knew God was using my gifts and the lessons I learned to help others. The planning of this conference kept me busy and helped me turn my obsession of being in a relationship into passion about fulfilling my purpose in Christ. Every week 50 to 80 singles and non-singles gathered in a small ballroom to watch Andy Stanley's *New Rules of Love Sex and Dating* series followed by lively and interactive conversation. Planning a conference may or may not be for you, but I assure you there is a gift that God is waiting to birth in you. He just wants you to commit to giving your all to him.

Getting involved in your local church also helps to surround you with like-minded individuals that can support your commitment versus criticizing it as a 'radical' decision. Getting involved in my local church helped me to grow my spiritual gifts while surrounding myself with people who provided encouragement on the difficult days.

Next Steps

If you realized that you do suffer from past hurt and struggle with one or several issues, as a single, you might be sitting there contemplating the one year challenge. If this is you, I want you to pray about this decision. I want you to ask God seriously how you can apply the above summary of the things you should work on during this year of your life. God has a beautiful love story for you. If this is a step He is encouraging you to take, trust that He will give you the strength to see you through.

Growth Exercise:

1. Evaluate the following areas and pray about, if and how, God is asking you to bring restoration to these areas of your life: Parental Relationships, Finances, Local Church Activities & the Breaking of Bad Habits.

2. Evaluate if you feel led to take the one year challenge and if the answer is yes; take out a calendar and mark one year from now and label it RESUME DATING!

Chapter 6
I'm Single, Now What?

When you are used to dating or simply just having someone in your life, it takes your mind a while to wrap around the fact that if you accept this challenge that person (or people) will no longer be there. I honestly believe one of the reasons I spent a year and a half trying to fix a relationship I broke, was because I didn't know what it was like to do life without him. I didn't know what it was, not to be able to call him, share a joke with him, run an idea by him or even see him. So when God said I need you to be single, I said, "Fine, Now WHAT??"

As a single person, a lot of us tend to have moments where we feel that God has forgotten about us. Society has taught us to view our season of singleness as a curse or a disease. I once told a friend of mine, we need to stop viewing married life as a 'better' life and simply view it as a different life. If we keep telling ourselves life will be so much 'better' when I can share it with someone which means that we are telling God, my life isn't good now, because you haven't given me someone. Thinking your life will only be better if you have someone is a lie that Satan wants you to believe. Your life can be as beautiful as you want it to be whether you are single or married, so simply embrace it!

We have to remind ourselves that we are here on earth to chase purpose, not people.

We have to remind ourselves that we are here on earth to chase purpose, not people. God knows the desires of our hearts. He sees our tears, and He wants us to know He has a great purpose for us. He just needs us to take our mind off of our obsession and turn it to our passion. If you have ever said to yourself, I'm single, now what? My answer is I've simply learned to live…

As a single person, I said to myself, I don't know if I can take a whole year off and risk my chances of not being able to get married anytime soon. However, the real question was, am I prepared to risk my chances of never marrying the right person? I said "Kerel, do you want a diamond and a party or a Christ-centered marriage with your partner in purpose?"

The start of my challenge was a struggle because I questioned myself a lot. I was 'technically' single for a year and a half before I began the year challenge, I thought "shouldn't that count for something?" However when I was honest with myself, I didn't spend that time as a single person preparing my mind, body and soul for the person God chose for me, so no, it didn't count. Getting in the mind frame to be completely single for a year was a scary thought. But, the last thing I wanted to do was wake up in the middle of a marriage and regret not taking the time I needed to prepare. Only you can answer if you truly spent that time as a single person growing into who God called you to be.

"A whole year, though, is it really that serious?" I once had a friend ask me. My answer was, "Yeah it is". I believe that God gives us choices and free will. This choice means we can accept His plan A for our life, or we could choose B, C, or D. So yes, I could have taken plan B. I did have options and good men who wanted to pursue me, but I chose to do it the way God wanted me to do it. I could have skipped the year challenge and married that great guy who did want me to be his wife. However, I knew I was broken; I knew I wasn't over my ex, and I knew I wasn't where God wanted me to be. I would have been no good to that man and no good to my marriage. You see when you accept Christ; you have this strong desire to do His plan for your life. Our plans may seem easier, but God's plan will always be better. His plan requires growth and change, and though the decision wasn't easy, it was the best decision for me.

I was scared of the change, but it was something I needed to do. If we don't have seasonal changes, our plants won't grow. As a single man, I believe there are steps that are required of you to be the man God called you to be. Although you may have many choices, God wants you to be completely whole when He introduces you to the woman He kept for you.

Ladies, if you have found yourself often singing the song "Oh woe is me." I want to encourage you to embrace this season; God is using it to stretch you. Stop making every conversation about "Where is my Boaz?" and be purposely single, not thirsty! Philippians 4:11 says "I am not saying this because I am in need, for I have learned whatever the circumstances to be content." You don't have to keep asking God where is he? We must learn to ask God what He requires of us during this season so that we can be content, purposeful, prepared and fruitful.

Many married women say that "marriage is one of the most selfless acts you can ever enter into, and if you're not ready for servanthood, you're not ready for marriage." God is using this season to prune us. As a common practice I have told myself, as long as you have no relationship, it means there is more work for you to do during this season. This season is for preparation: Luke 16:10 (NIV), "Unless you are faithful in small matters you won't be faithful in large matters". Stay quiet at the feet of Christ and be open to His directions.

Growth Exercise:

1. If you know you keep putting off taking the time to get closer to God, sit and ask God to reveal the things in your life that seem to difficult to give up and ask Him to show you how to do life His way.

2. Men: Watch Pastor Myles Munroe's You-Tube Sermon "Five Characteristics of the Ideal Man" and evaluate how these steps apply to your current season of singleness.

3. Ladies: Watch Janette's "I will wait for you" You-Tube clip and evaluate how her poem can serve as an encouragement for you during this season of singleness.

Chapter 7
Fall in Love with God

After I decided to accept the one year challenge, I knew the only way I could make it through an entire year of not dating was by choosing to stay at the feet of Christ. They said that prayer changes things, and I was finally ready for a change. I had been a Christian from the time I was eight years old, but if I was honest I never really took the time to know who God was. My life was about acknowledging Him, not learning how to please Him. So I wanted to learn. I often heard the phrase, "A woman after God's own heart" and wondered if I would ever be capable of being this kind of woman.

When I think of a woman after God's own heart, my heart immediately remember the Master Class episode story I watched on Oprah Winfrey and how she surrendered her life to God. Long before the celebrated *Oprah Winfrey Show* and the OWN network, Oprah Winfrey had a childhood dream of being an actress. At the tender age of fourteen, she developed an affinity with the novel *The Color Purple*. Realizing that this story so closely embodied her present reality, she felt a deep connection to this novel, reading it cover-to-cover and sharing the book with all of her friends.

Years later, Oprah was filled with excitement when she learned that Steven Spielberg would be producing the movie *The Color Purple*.

She auditioned for the role in anticipation, but weeks passed with no call. She called the casting director and he scolded her for calling and insulted her lack of experience. She was devastated. She thought how could God bring her this far to leave her? In her moment of defeat, she asked God to take her desire to play the role away. If it wasn't meant to be she wanted to genuinely accept God's will for her life. She cried and cried that day as she surrendered her will but eventually she felt peace. Moments after that peace she got a phone call from Steven Spielberg telling her she got the role.

God's not looking for perfection, He's just looking for complete submission to His will. She couldn't believe it! At that moment, she watched God totally show up. Sometimes when you release it to God, He will release it to you! This story is a true reflection of God's grace for us when we devote our heart to Him. Having a heart for God doesn't mean you're perfect, take a look at the story in the Bible of David. David was a man after God's own heart, but he was also an adulterer and a murderer. God's not looking for perfection, He's just looking for complete submission to His will.

God showed up for Oprah that day. However, my favorite part of the story isn't the part where God rewarded her with the role. My favorite part comes when she desperately prayed the prayer to let go of her agenda for her life and the peace God granted her at that moment. Having peace in the midst of disappointment is one of the greatest gifts we can ever receive. There is a beauty in letting go of our plans and casting those cares to Jesus. Can you do that? Can you imagine someone else in the movie role you wanted? Can you imagine someone else receiving the award you worked so hard for or could you imagine someone else marrying the person your heart refuses to let go? Can you watch that? Can you see that and be genuinely happy to surrender your will to Christ, because sometimes that's what God requires us to do.

Oprah's story reminds us that God can dream a bigger dream for you, than you can ever dream for yourself. She thought her role in *The Color Purple* was the pinnacle moment of her career. She didn't even realize that it was just a stepping stone for all of the greatness that was about to unfold.

To be a true woman or man after God's own heart, you have to be willing to let go of you. Yes, we all have dreams and desires, and a lot of those are put there by Christ. Therefore it's important to have a dream, to do the work, to pray to God, but after that it's even more important to let go of it all and simply give it back to Christ. Oprah reminds us that when you have done all you can, work, strive, plead, bargained and hope, JUST surrender it to God. Give it up to the One that is greater than you.

I know getting to that place where I turned my desires to God and gave Him the final say is great in theory but harder in reality. So if you have thought this way before, you are right, being completely obedient and surrendered to Christ won't happen overnight. But, I have found that the journey is easier when you commit yourself to building a stronger relationship with God one day at a time. My intimacy grew with God when I surrendered my life to do the following things:

Listen to God: Read my Bible

When you're on your journey to discovering a deeper relationship with God, you struggle with the question, "Can I hear from God for myself?" For years I battled with certain desires, asking if these desires are what God wants or desires I want. That's why Oprah's story resonated with me so much; she shares the important lesson that if it's truly a God thing, we can let it go. When you can take your eyes off the obsession and make it all about Christ, you are one step closer to identifying God's voice in your life.

I know there are times when I directly heard from God, and He showed Himself to me. And, I also know that there were other times when I felt I heard God, but it was my voice pushing my personal agenda. We must learn to have a conversation with God daily, and when we read His Word, we will be able to recognize His voice.

I'll admit growing up I saw the Bible as a boring book, and I had no motivation to read it. At this point in life, some of us may still have days that we feel this way. Or maybe you are at a point that I was a few years ago when I decided to read devotionals and inspirational novels, and only open my Bible during Sunday morning service. The Holy Spirit soon convicted me with the reminder that no matter how many great books you read, these will NEVER substitute for reading the Word of God for yourself. When I realized this revelation, I made it a daily practice to try my best to add reading my Bible to my everyday devotion. John 8:47 (NIV) says, "He who belongs to God hears, what God says." I believe we hear the voice of God by reading His Word.

So if you are hungry to hear what God says, open His Word. Maybe you are struggling with trusting God when He is telling you to do something that doesn't seem to make any sense. If you are, read the story of Joshua and how he led the Israelites into the Promised Land. God asked the Israelites to walk around the city of Jericho for seven days and on the seventh day He asked them to walk around seven times. This instruction may seem crazy to you, and it probably seemed crazy to them, but God knew what He was doing. Sometimes I wonder what if they stopped walking on the sixth day, right before their breakthrough? They wholeheartedly served for years before God granted what He had for them. So sometimes we serve and can't figure out, Lord, how long must I be faithful? Be reminded God's promises to you will be fulfilled. But it has to be in God's time.

Over a month ago, when I was asked not to come back to work until further notice, my heart was filled with panic. This huge hotel project where I was working was being put on hold, and we were told to go home indefinitely. The whole thing still seems unbelievable. A lot of my co-workers ran to job interviews in fear of what seemed like the inevitable; eventually losing our jobs and no longer being paid. Instead for me, during this time God told me I gave you this time to write. So when people would ask me what was my next move? Where did I apply? What I was going to do once the payments stopped? I simply replied, "God did not give me permission to apply anywhere, He simply told me just to write."

Even hearing myself say it, sounds a little crazy. But when you are constantly reading the Word of God you know that there are times when He told his servants to do things that seemed crazy but in

His time he revealed His plan for their life. Sometimes God's plan is just for us to be obedient to His will. The simple fact that you can read this book is a testimony of what God was calling me to do during this season. He knew I couldn't finish it on my 9 to 5, so He let me go and took care of my finances in the meantime. Won't He do it! He is waiting to reveal His will to you; He just wants you to open His Word so that you can be intimate with Him.

Journal / Meditation

Reading the Bible is the way God talks to you and journaling is a way I believe you can to talk to God. Two years ago, I wrote that by March 27th, 2016 I would have completed my second Master's degree. The night after I wrote that prophecy, I found a school that had the exact field I wanted to study. Two years later I sit here, two courses away from finishing by the winter of 2015. God is good!

One of the best things about journaling is it serves as a private timeline of growth and restoration. You get to reflect on areas where you have grown and areas where you still may struggle. It's also amazing to watch God's answered prayers take form right before your eyes after days, weeks and when you reflect on your journal entries sometimes even years down the road, you are able to see your growth. Journaling every day has helped to strengthen my daily communication with my Heavenly Father. If you are interested in developing a better journaling habit, see my ten tips below that will help you on your journey.

10 Tips for Journal Time with God:

1. Get a cute or colorful cover that makes you excited to write every day. A lot of journals also have an inspirational message or scripture on their cover; this helps to serve as a reminder of your purpose for writing.

2. Place it on the nightstand by your bed, so you are reminded every morning or evening to write your thoughts.

3. What to write: Anything and everything, ideas, revelations, inspirations, dreams, goals, visions, or something significant that happened to you that day or the day before.

4. Journaling is also a way to talk to God. Tell him when you are angry, sad, happy, excited, overwhelmed. Write down your prayer requests and silent petitions.

5. Journal EVERY DAY.

6. Remember the length of the entry is totally up to you!

7. Making notes from a really good book that you may be reading at the time is a good way to keep records of the author's ideas that you thought were insightful.

8. Keep it sacred, don't turn it into a book for grocery list, gossip or allow someone else to use it.

9. Sometimes it helps the flow of your thoughts to journal to gospel or inspirational music.

10. Remember to date every entry as a reminder of how you are feeling at that time of year. You will be amazed to see your progress over the years.

Spiritual Music

What you feed your spirit through music is so important. Because it can draw you closer to your fleshly desires or it could draw you closer to God. I remember when I was going through my first real break up. I started to listen to songs like T*he First Cut is the Deepest*, *I'll Never Fall in Love Again*, and *How Could an Angel Break my Heart?*. At that moment, I was ignorantly spewing evil thoughts against my life and future relationships. I was telling my heart that I was experiencing the deepest pain I would ever have and that I would never learn to love that hard again, scary right?

When we feed our spirit with certain words, we are putting a curse over ourselves. Years later we sit and ponder why I have had so many failed or dysfunctional relationships? When the truth is, our relationships fail because we have spent so much time speaking against healthy ones. Proverbs 18:21 (NIV) says, "The tongue has the power of life and death, and those who love it will eat its fruit."

God is not looking to attract your problems; God wants to attract your praise.

God is not looking to attract your problems; God wants to attract your praise. Trust God to direct your musical interests. I want to encourage you to ask Him, "Does this edify You, does this bring You glory, is this preparing me for who You called me to be?" If the answer is no, let it go. Songs like *To Worship You I Live*, *Fill Me Up* and *I'll Trust You Lord* help to speak life to you. Use your tongue to fill your spirit with God's truth instead of the lies of this world.

If you want true intimacy with God, watch what you feed your spirit, because what you feed you spirit is eventually what your soul will believe. *I'm in love with the Co, Co* has a really hot beat but is that really what you want to be feeding your spirit? Usher may not mind that he has a stripper for a girlfriend but is that what you want for your friends, your daughters or yourself? If not, don't allow the beat to fool you. Everyone has a right to choose their musical playlist. However I can assure you the more you fill your spirit with the lyrics that edify your Heavenly Father the more you will grow in intimacy with Him. I truly believe the dependency of your growth rests in the hands of the music you choose.

Serving

I mentioned previously how serving in your local church is a great place to grow your spiritual gifts and surround yourself with other like-minded individuals. Also, it's important to note that serving helps to build your intimacy with Christ. Joshua 24:14 (NIV) says, "Now therefore fear the LORD and serve him with sincerity and faithfulness. Put away the gods that your fathers served beyond the River and in Egypt, and serve the LORD". When we serve God out of obligation or duty, we fail, but when we serve God out of love, we succeed.

A lot of times when we hear the testimonies of women who 'prepared' themselves to be found by their husband, they often say, "I got super busy in my church and joined all kinds of ministries and just like that, he was there!" Now don't get me wrong, but I honestly cringe every time I hear this statement and here is why. Single women who have a strong desire to be married as I mentioned in my introduction are sometimes vulnerable to falling into the trap of wanting a 'formula' to finding their husband.

Believe me when I say there is no formula. You cannot find your husband, it's your husband's job to find you. God doesn't grant you a husband because of your works. He introduces you to your mate, at His appropriate time, because it's a part of your purpose.

I would encourage Christian married women to be sure to clarify the statement of exactly what they mean when they say, "I simply got super busy in various church ministries until I found my husband." I say this because although your motives may be pure, some single women interpret this to mean, getting super busy in the church will get me a man. As a single woman or man, your busyness in various ministries shouldn't be done as a distraction or a way to gain brownie points with God. God doesn't want you to serve because you are using it as a bargaining tool. He wants you to serve because it is a reflection of your love for Him. God wants you to serve because He knows certain ministries will help to give growth to the purpose He has already built inside of you. James 4:8, "Draw nigh to God and he will draw near to you". It's easy to fall into this trap, so now and then I took myself to a quiet place and gave God permission to check my motives. We should serve because we love Him, not because we want something from Him.

Giving

If I am honest, this is a level of intimacy with God that I am desperately trying to improve. As I mentioned, I struggled with selfishness for a long time, so giving does not come naturally to me. However, I do know that God requires it. It would be easier to grow in the intimacy with God if we learned that showing love to others, is a way of showing our love to God.

Matthew 25:39-40 (NIV) says, "When did we see you sick, or in prison, and come to you? The King will answer and say to them. Truly I say to you, to the extent that you did it to one of these brothers of mine, even the least of them, you did it to me." I don't want God to turn me away because I refused to exercise a giving spirit. Like a lot of people, I have hosted an event and given a portion of proceeds to charity. Still, I have often wondered what a difference it would make if I made a daily commitment to spend more time genuinely giving into someone's life?

Giving can take place in various forms. We can give someone our time, our words of affirmation, free use of our talents or gifts or monetary donation. I tend to be a big fan of symbiotic relationships. Yet, that's not truly giving because you know at the end of the day, there is something in it for you. That's not giving, that's business. True giving is when you give into the life of someone you know could never repay you for your gift. An anonymous encouraging card on your neighbor's door, food stamps taped to the bottom of pampers in a food store. Making a scholarship donation to your former high school or spending the afternoon at the children's hospital are all ways that you can give into the lives of others without expecting anything in return. When we truly love someone, we are willing to give them our last. If you love God and want to be intimate with Him, we must be willing to give into those around us.

Prayer Life

Praying to God will also grow your intimacy with Him. We should pray: not only to ask for things but more importantly to ask God what we can do for Him. Proverbs 16:2-3 (NIV), "A man's way may seem innocent to him, but God weighs motives. Commit to the Lord whatever you do and your plans will succeed". When we pray, we shouldn't be asking God to fulfill our selfish desires, we should be asking Him to make us open, willing and able to fulfill the plans that He has created for us.

When I was still living with my parents, they made the suggestion that they wanted to pray every morning before work. At first I thought, oh great, now I'm going to be late for work. We were told to pray prayers of gratitude. Thanking God for the things He had done and thanking Him in advance for the things He would do. I thanked God for the success of my play, my trip to Italy and my new job all before they manifested themselves as a reality in my life. But more importantly I gave God permission only to bless me with the things that were a part of His purpose for my life.

God encourages us to come to Him in prayer to worship Him and to thank Him for everything He has already done. A lot of times we try to fix or make things happen on our own, especially when we are praying for someone else. However, God gives us the power of prayer because sometimes that's the only thing He wants us to do. When things become overwhelming, God encourages us to cast our cares upon Him, so that we may understand that anything and everything we do is a result of His grace and mercy in our life. God encourages us to fight our battle through prayer because we wrestle not against flesh or blood but spiritual warfare. I do not understand everything about spiritual warfare, but I know it's real. Therefore, no matter how angry or disappointed I get, the best way I know how to fight my battle is on my knees.

Fasting

Fasting is a word that may scare some of us because so many times the focus is on the lack of food and Lord knows 'we love some FOOD'. The purpose of fasting should be to take your eyes off the things of this world, to focus completely on God. People usually fast when they are looking to God for a breakthrough in their life. If they are trying to break an addiction or if they are praying to God for the salvation of a loved one, someone may go on a fast. Sometimes people fast to be simply able to hear the voice of God more clearly. Getting quiet to hear Christ and resisting the pleasures of the world can bring you to the most intimate place with God.

Therefore, it could be taking a break from anything you do too much of. I'm a social media 'junkie', so I usually refrain from Instagram and Facebook when I fast, along with the denial of food. Maybe your sweet addiction is football or a morning fix of a small vanilla latte. Whatever it is that you choose to give up; God will reward your sacrifice.

My suggestion if you have never fasted before is to start with a fasting period that you can manage; for example, having only liquids and not eating until 12 p.m. or until three p.m for that week, or just one day of liquids. It's also important to remember that it's not a mandatory practice to be a Christian. It's completely voluntary and geared towards growing your faith in Christ. Christians fast as a way to demonstrate to God, and to ourselves, that we are serious about

> You can't make a demand on God without Him making a demand on you.

our relationship with Him. Fasting tells God: "There is nothing and no one more important to me than You." It helps us to gain a new perspective and a renewed reliance upon God. You can't make a demand on God without Him making a demand on you.

Commit to Change, Submission, and Solitude

When you know that you are here for something bigger and greater, it feels weird to be in a setting where you can't be the light that God has called you to be. When you are intimate with God, there is a fear you feel when you aren't doing right. Like when you were sneaking out to the place, you know the place your parents told you, you shouldn't be. I remember standing in night clubs and certain kinds of parties, after committing to a life of ministry and feeling like a fish out of the water. Everyone has their personal journey to travel, but for me, the Holy Spirit wanted to let me know it was time for a change. For years being in this setting, felt like second nature, but for some reason, my stomach now rejected this setting and God was telling me to run. God was getting ready to set me up and being set up and set apart comes with a certain level of change. God wants us to pass the test.

Submission to God's will isn't always easy. It's a conscious decision for you to say, "Take my will and conform it to you Lord." If God says I don't want you to apply to any jobs right now, as scary as this season is for me, I have to trust God. I can't waste my time applying because it's what everyone else is doing. I have to submit to God.

A lot of independent women run from the word submission, but I embrace it. It was funny to me when a young lady I went to college with was outraged because of a post I shared on my Facebook account. The post of a blog stating "I have no problem submitting to my husband." She couldn't believe it. I was an educated, well-traveled, and established young woman living in the 21st century and admitting that I would submit to my future husband...I sure was!

You see the thing is, submission isn't hard for me to grasp because I had already begun to submit my will to Christ. I don't make one move without consulting Jesus, who is my covering. I learned the hard way that when you try to move before God is ready, it's not going to happen. He's going to block it. Therefore when I get married, I will also consult my husband, who will also consult Christ. I'm not afraid to submit to a man who is being led by Christ. I also know that God won't ever bless me with that opportunity if I don't first learn to submit to Him.

Change and submission can be a painful process and, therefore, the growth of the acceptance of this should be done in solitude. Time alone with God helps to cement your intimacy. Don't be afraid to be alone with God and your thoughts. If you truly are seeking to be a man or woman after God's own heart, your prayer life can't only consist of asking God to help you pass a test. And it can't just be so God can find you a husband or wife or get you a new job. Your growth takes place when you learn to read God's Word every day. Deepen your prayer life, fast, serve, give, listen, meditate, change and submit to Christ's will for you. He desperately wants to be intimate with you, He's ready to take your relationship to a new level, and He's just waiting for you.

Growth Exercise:

1. Go out and buy your first journal or pick back up one you intended to use at one time and begin to document your journey through Christ.

2. List in your journal at least one thing from this chapter that God is encouraging you to do to grow closer to Him.

PREPARATION

Chapter 8
Growth is Everything

Often when I tell others that I decided to take a year off from dating, by no surprise, their first question is usually, "Why?" After I tell them why, I continue to explain that "my ONE year of NO dating was challenging!!" But seriously, "It was also beautiful, hard, humbling, but most of all, it was filled with growth." One of my mantras that I live by is: "Growth is everything."

1 Corinthians 13:11 (NIV) says, "When I was a child, I talked like a child; I thought like a child, I reasoned like a child. When I became a man, I put the ways of childhood behind me." The year I began my year challenge changed me for the better. It was the year I made a conscious decision to put my childish ways behind me. It didn't happen overnight and even today I am still by no means perfect, I think it's safe to say that I will never be perfect. However, I'm simply an ordinary girl striving to live the life that God wants for me.

At the beginning of my year, there was no step-by-step guideline of what I should expect. I honestly think this journey will look different for every single person that decides to embrace it. Despite the fact that there were no general guidelines on what I should do, with all of this new found freedom and energy, there were some things that I explored that made this journey to growth a little easier.

Read More Books

"Great books help you understand, and they help you feel understood."- John Green. On one of the first days of my journey, I decided that if I was going to navigate my way through to getting closer to God, I wanted to hear the stories of others who had faced life's struggles, stories that were relatable to my experience. So I went to our local Christian bookstore, not knowing many Christian authors at the time and just decided to pray about my decision. At this point in my life, I went to church every Sunday, but I couldn't tell you who a 'mega pastor' was, which women were leading international ministries, and I definitely couldn't tell you who was writing any Christian books. Besides my usual Joyce Meyer's devotional and an occasional good old drama/love story novel I borrowed from my sister, I wouldn't have considered myself an avid reader.

Despite my lack of knowledge of Christian authors and books with a Christian theme, something in me said that this was a good place to start. So as I paced through the aisles, I suddenly came across a book that had an attractive, caucasian woman on the cover with the biggest smile on her face. For some reason, her smile was inviting, and the bright orange and blue background of her cover also helped to draw me in. But, it was her title that officially sealed the deal: ***He Loves Me; He Loves Me Not*** *– What Every Woman Needs to Know About Unconditional Love, but Is Afraid to Feel.* WOW, that title hit me like a ton of bricks, and I would be lying if I didn't say that my mind didn't immediately go to my ex when I saw it. How could it not, this is the question I had been asking myself for the last year and a half: "I wonder if He still loves me or if He loves me not?" The Holy Spirit then gave me the 'heads up' that this book was about Christ and not a man, and that I needed to focus.

I decided then that regardless of who it was referring to, I wanted to know unconditional love. I wanted to know the kind of love that understood that we are all imperfect people. I wanted to know about a love that believed in second chances. I wanted to know what it felt like for God to love me unconditionally. So I grabbed the book and decided, this is where I would start.

The author of this book happens to be world renowned preacher Paula White. In the store that day, to me, she was just a woman with an inviting cover and title. But a few days later she became the first famous spiritual leader whose story I connected to and for that, I will be forever grateful. It was amazing when God gave me the opportunity to meet her in person, during a session this summer, at T.D. Jakes' Mega Fest. Our meeting was brief, as there was a line of people waiting to greet her as well. But I was just happy that I got to tell her thank you for writing the first book that I read, when I made the decision to rediscover my spiritual journey.

He Loves Me; He Loves Me Not invited readers into Paula's life story, one filled with divorce, second chances and the opportunity to discover God's love for her. I connected to her story because she didn't pretend to be perfect, she was honest about the broken areas of her life and confessed how God still loved her unconditionally. Paula's testimony forced me to look at the broken areas of my life by confronting the opposition that was keeping me away from the blessings that God wanted to give me. Through this book, I learned about what real unconditional love felt like, and that kind of love that can only come from God. I learned as humans we must understand and accept the love from God first, before we place expectations of love on others.

After completing this book, a true bookworm was born, and I was ready to take on what was next. A friend of mine then introduced me to Heather Lindsay and bought me her first book as a gift to me, *Pink Lips and Empty Hearts*. This book was very down-to-earth and relatable. I felt like she was telling my life story through her eyes and it began to wreck my spirit even more. I'll never forget the line that did it for me, "Run from that man who is confused about you, your husband will know you and know the purpose for you in his life." It was like a light bulb went off in my head. If something is for me, it will never miss me, and if it misses me, it was never for me.

Sometimes we have to learn to walk away, because we're waiting on an answer from a person, instead of waiting on an answer from God. Sometimes God has already told us to walk away and that person's silence or confusion is confirming it. Heather Lindsay's book then became a springboard to starting a book club. This book club helped me to discover and read more books by authors like Andy Stanley, John Maxwell, Dr. Myles Munroe, Cornelius Lindsey and Ravi Zacharias to give a few names.

Reading was not only a great past time to keep my mind off dating during that year. The lessons I learned on purpose, leadership, God's grace and relationships also had an extreme impact on my growth moving forward. My favorite kinds of books are books filled with testimonies and encourage self-development, but I also have read great fiction novels that possess great messages on love, life, and growth. One of my favorite fiction writers is Emily Giffin. She has a great gift of telling stories that impact the heart. Making a choice to read more during that year was one of the best decisions I could ever make.

Discover New Talents, Interest, and Gifts

I have always been a very active person. So when I began my one year challenge, I was already involved in a few projects. I was in the middle of completing my first online reality show, *The New Face of Mango Tree Media* and I was still in my first year as the Chairperson for my sorority's mentoring initiative: The Twenty Pearls program. Even with all those projects going on, I still wanted to make myself available to God to develop new opportunities in my life. So when my mom asked me to be one of the leaders of the first ever 'small groups' ministry that my church was hosting, I willingly agreed. I had always considered myself a leader, but I don't think before I entered this season of my life I would have been willing to lead a Christian small group. I always considered myself a Christian but as you have read, my life didn't always align with how I was supposed to live. And even worse, before now, I wasn't actively trying to make a change, so I never quite felt led to do something on this level. However, this new commitment to a one year challenge was all about making the effort to live my life God's way, so I thought that leading this group would also be a great start.

So eventually I started hosting a weekly small group and monthly book club at my house. This book club is where I discovered my love for teaching others about God's love and the art of entertaining guests. I also loved baking cookies or preparing meals for my guests, rather than just serving snacks and store bought cupcakes. As I mentioned in a previous chapter, you don't have to wait to be in a relationship to learn to enjoy cooking, serving and entertaining others. This season allowed me to develop my skills by showing Christ's love to others. It also really helped to break down some of my strong selfish behaviors that I held on to for years.

During this season, I also rediscovered my love for writing. I had always had an interest in writing after I wrote my first short play in 2010. At that time, it was just something new that I wanted to try and I never quite got back into the swing of it until 2013. I had a strong push from the Holy Spirit to begin a blog during the summer of my one year challenge, but I was nervous about actually being able to do it. Would people want to listen to what I had to say and if I started it, did I have the level of commitment needed to be consistent? By this time, I had begun to follow a few blogs, and although they were inspiring, they never seemed to be consistent. The people I was following got caught up in their daily lives and months would soon pass without being able to read one of their new entries. I wanted to be consistent, so I decided I would blog once a month and that my outline for my first year would focus on the nine fruits of the spirit. Not only did this become an attainable goal, but I am also now at the beginning of my third year as a blogger. In my blog, I got the opportunity to be transparent about my struggles, triumphs, and journey. When I would receive Facebook inbox messages or emails about how much my blog had touched someone's life, I knew I was beginning to step into my calling.

During this year as I mentioned, I also hosted my first four week conference, entitled *The New Rules of Love, Sex, and Dating*. And I once again got involved in my local theater by performing the role of Rizzo in my favorite musical, Grease.

As you can see staying positively active was a true goal of mine during this year. I also found a greater appreciation for gospel concerts, having the opportunity to hear from the ministry of Tasha Cobbs, Jonathan Nelson, William Murphy, and Preshea Hillard. The crazy thing is before that year I had no idea who these singers were. But when I opened myself up to new possibilities, God began to not only transform my heart, He transformed my focus. He was nurturing my passions and gifts without me even knowing it. I was beginning to be who God called me to be.

> When I opened myself up to new possibilities, God began to not only transform my heart, He transformed my focus.

Education

For me, education can take place in many different forms. I love learning something new every day and as 'cheesy' as it may sound, as long as I live I never want to stop learning. Whether I am attending a workshop, seminar, doing a summer course or taking on an entirely new degree, for me knowledge is power. So even though I had a lot of side eyes when I decided to start my second Master's degree in Communications and Leadership, I didn't regret it. I truly believe my second degree got me a new job and gave me the courage to break out of a profession where I had spent eight years, but didn't love.

The New Rules of Love, Sex and Dating was one of the first experiences where I had listened to a sermon that was not only insightful but extremely interesting. After a while, I was watching sermons more than I had ever watched TV. It was surprising to me how much I enjoyed them. Most people enjoy a little good, televised word on a Sunday morning, but this became a two to three times a week habit for me. Andy Stanley got me hooked on to his natural ability to be such an effective communicator. For me, he wasn't like those old fashioned preachers that you fell asleep on every Sunday morning, especially after getting home late from the club. Andy was real, relaxed and comfortable. I took my journal out every time I would watch a new video. I learned so much about what it meant to have a real relationship with God during this season. I spent a whole lot of free time watching his sermons and learning about other preachers with a similar style. Now some of my other favorite preachers to listen to are Joyce Meyer, Toure Roberts, Sarah Jakes, T.D. Jakes and Joel Osteen.

Sermons weren't the only thing I was running to for growth. I found that workshops and seminars were also very helpful to me. While at my sorority's leadership conference that summer, I went to a workshop that focused on developing a greater self-awareness. We had to do an exercise where we listed our favorite quote, scripture, symbol, place and song that defined who we were as a person. These things crossed my mind before, but it heightened my level of self-awareness, when in a moment you were challenged to tell the person next to you the name of the song that speaks to the very core of who you are as a person.

It was also during this workshop, I learned about and made a decision to make my very first vision board. When the conference was over, this was a project that kept me motivated and busy over the next few weeks. I filled my board up with photos and symbols of places I would love to go and people I would love to one day work with or meet. Those people also symbolized goals I wanted to accomplish. Since I began my vision board in 2013, there are some visions that I had the privilege to see come to light. I got the opportunity to not only meet Meagan Good and DeVon Franklin but the chance to do an on-stage interview and spend time with them during an entire conference weekend.

I had learned about their story when flipping through a magazine during the summer while putting together my vision board. I had never even thought about putting them on there but I was so intrigued by their story, I began to Google their journey. I found out that DeVon had written a book, was mentored under Will Smith and T.D. Jakes and also was the producer of movies like the *Karate Kid* and *The Pursuit of Happiness*. I read his book and watched most of his online interviews and placed them on my board as a couple whose partnership in Christ I hoped to one day emulate. I knew I would love to meet and work with them one day, but I never dreamed that it would happen so soon. I still remember the day an old high school friend asked me to join the committee for her church that was bringing Meagan and DeVon to Freeport, Bahamas to speak. I couldn't believe it. I had placed it on my vision board, a little less than a year ago, and there I was sitting in the middle of an answered prayer. So, write the vision, make it plain.

I truly believe the faith that you place on a vision board will work. I also eventually moved into a home on my own, started a successful business, traveled to Italy and became a healthier person. I also got to hear T.D. Jakes, Joyce Meyer, and Tyler Perry all speak in person this past summer at MegaFest. These spiritual leaders were also on my vision board. However, they will remain on my list until I also have the chance to one day meet or work with them in person as well. #faithworks

So whether you decide to take a new computer class, learn to crochet, or travel to learn a new language, this season is worth expanding your growth.

Travel

Traveling is without a shadow of doubt one of my favorite things to do. My mother always says that most people feel that they don't have any money, but she believes that most people do have money; everyone just chooses to place their money on the things they value. So if you are up to your neck in student loans, it's because you value education, and you're using the money you obtain to pay for one or more degrees. For me, I know for sure that I value education and travel. I will spend money on things that help me grow and things that help me to see the world.

During the summer of 2013, I scheduled three back-to-back trips starting in Montreal, then North Carolina and then on to Jamaica. I called it my mini "eat, pray, love" summer vacation. The city of Montreal was where my sorority was holding their leadership conference, and we were there for five days for an unbelievable experience. I got the chance to meet new sorority sisters from all over the world, explore the city with my mother and learn so much from the various leadership workshops that I attended. My favorite night in Montreal happened when all of the members from the Bahamas decided to walk down to a local spot that had a variety of food truck vendors. I went to several different vendors trying foods from all over the world while we sat on the steps of an outdoor arena and watched their cultural show. It was a beautiful afternoon where we got the chance to share in laughter, great conversation and enjoy some really good food. As a true foodie, I can still remember how great it felt to bask at that moment. This experience made a great start to my mini vacation.

I then went on to my sister's house in North Carolina for two weeks simply as a means to get away. By this time, I was in the middle of my year challenge, and I needed to be in a quiet place to regroup. The time I spent here I mostly worked on my vision board, rested and wrote my play *Sarah's Wedding*. Overall I just wanted a break from being surrounded by others. I wanted to have the chance to get quiet in the presence of Christ, and so that's what I did.

I ended my "eat, pray, love" vacation at one of my best friend's wedding in Jamaica. It was a beautiful experience to stand by her side as they pledged the rest of their lives to each other. That weekend I got a chance to reunite with high school friends, climb Dunn's River Falls and enjoy the cool breeze of Jamaica while sipping on pina coladas on the beach of the resort. It was a weekend to remember!

In all of these experiences, my favorite part of the trip was the rehearsal dinner. During that time, they allowed everyone present to go around and share kind words about the bride and groom. Everyone had funny stories and great words of affirmation to share, but it was even more amazing to see the kind words that the groom's family all had to share about the bride, my friend. They told stories of how she made everyone laugh the first time they met her and how the groom would be in trouble if he ever did anything to hurt her. He jokingly started to question if his family, actually loved her more than they loved him. You could tell that she didn't only win the heart of her soon-to-be husband, she had also captured the love of his entire family. That moment reminded me that in the right time, love can truly be a beautiful thing.

Taking time away from my everyday routine to spend it with family and friends was exactly what the doctor ordered. My "eat, pray love" was a success and the perfect get away for that year. Even after my year was complete, travel remains ingrained in my very soul. Every year I try to keep the promise I made to myself to always visit somewhere new. Whether it's a new island, new city, new state or even new country, I never want to stop traveling to the beauty found in the other cultures around me.

Understanding Me

As my one year challenge began to come to a close, I was interviewed on a friend's blog and was labeled as a "Woman to Watch." I was honored to be featured because the interview's aim was to touch the lives of the readers around me, in a hope to evoke change. But even more, to my surprise my responses simply helped me to minister to myself. I talked about my upcoming projects, my painful experiences and what I had hoped for the future. I had learned how to put Christ in the driver's seat of my life, and I was finally proud of the woman I was becoming. I was still a little tattered and wounded, but along the way my journey to wholeness was beginning to unfold right in front of me.

As I said before, there is no set-in-stone guideline of what and how many new things one should try when seeking to grow. I believe God made us all unique and different for a reason. Maybe things you began to think of as new talents or interests aren't even on the above list. The point is, it's so important to get to know you. Maybe you want to start a new sport, begin a new workout plan or volunteer at a senior living residence. Whatever it is, I think we all grow from trying something new. When I began to evaluate all of the things that I was able to accomplish it began to shock me. I had no clue how much time and energy went into wanting to be in a relationship. While dating, I would obsess over planning every detail for a wedding day, when I never even had a ring. I no longer wanted to be that kind of girl. Therefore, I had to change my interests because I was determined to grow.

Growth Exercise:

1. List five growing opportunities you always wanted to do but never took the time to do.

2. Set a date on your calendar for when you will start at least one of the activities on your above list.

Chapter 9
Growing Pains

I would be doing my experience an injustice if I didn't take the time to be honest with you about the struggles I faced during this year. My story isn't complete without the hard times. Believe me when I say walking away with the vision of all the amazing forms of growth also came with a lot of obstacles. You can't appreciate the essence of a dream fulfilled without knowing the hardships that came along the way. I have an endless list of dreams, and one of those dreams includes being blessed with a God-ordained marriage, where we push each other closer to Christ more than we push each other towards ourselves. However, great rewards require great sacrifices. So when times got hard, and, boy, did they get hard, I would always repeat to myself, "God never said it would be easy, He said it would be worth it!"

Loneliness

It's no surprise that this year can have its fair share of lonely days, and the truth is loneliness can take form in the simplest things. Sometimes no one is there to ask how your day was, stroke your hair or comfort your fears. During this year, no one was there to try a new romantic restaurant that I wanted to go to and though I could always go on my own, I sometimes really just wanted to save that restaurant experience for someone special and those days were hard.

Loneliness also gets harder during 'cuffing season'. For those who don't know what 'cuffing season' is, the Urban Dictionary defines "this season as a time that usually falls during the colder months of fall and winter". They describe this as a time when people are so cold that they are anxious to find someone to cuddle with and keep them warm. Well in the Bahamas it doesn't get that cold, but I would admit having someone warm next to me, did cross my mind a time or two.

Still, I think the hardest thing about cuffing season is all the holidays that fall during that time. Being single at Christmas, New Year's and Valentine's Day is easier on the pockets. However, you tend to have moments when you get "in your feelings" because you can think of thousands of ways you could spend this holiday with someone you love. But you can only come up with one or two on how you can spend it alone.

Birthdays can also be a sore point during this year because it may be the first birthday where you don't have a significant other showering you with beautiful words, a weekend getaway and lavish gifts. Sometimes it's just you planning something with your girls and praying it's a day to remember. My birthday fell shy of three months into my year challenge and at this point I had been doing pretty well on my journey. I felt confident about my growth, I was reading, staying busy and I had begun to learn that it didn't always have to be about me. So I didn't mind spending my entire birthday catering to one of my good friends/mentors on her wedding day. Yet halfway through the hustle and bustle of the day's coordination, things began to slow down and without the business to distract me, I was beginning to get depressed.

You know the "Woe is me, when will it be my wedding day." "Why did I do this stupid one year challenge?" kind of talk. Well, after one or two glasses of wine, I got depressed. I kept looking at my phone to see if my ex-boyfriend sent me a 'Happy Birthday' message. I shouldn't have even cared, but the truth is, I did. It was hard for me to move on knowing my life was no longer how it used to be. I had to realize in reality my life was different, and he had no obligation to call me and with that he never did.

I sulked the whole day and, needless to say, I was not proud of myself, but the truth is, you will have those days. James 1:2-4 (NIV) tells us, "Consider it pure joy whenever you face trials of many kinds because you know the testing of your faith, and faith develops perseverance and perseverance must finish its work so that you may be mature and complete."

I had to learn that my loneliness wouldn't be cured by running back to the same thing that brought me to my knees. I had to learn that my journey wasn't about anyone I dated in the past because they couldn't help me get to the place of wholeness that God was calling me to be. Whenever I refused to let go, God simply used their rejection to direct me back to Him. Sometimes God allows you to go through rejection and painful situations because He wants you to find your strength in Him. So after that day, I began to tell myself when loneliness begins to get the best of you, do your best to run to the throne, not to your phone.

Comparison Game

In this new age of social media, it's almost impossible not to have a moment of jealousy toward your friend or random classmate who you hardly ever talked to in high school. Despite this distant connection, this 'friend' is now in your Facebook news feed every day with their wedding countdown and 'kissy-face' selfies. I had to learn to accept that throughout this year, I would see people my age, get engaged, get married, have a baby, have two babies, celebrate anniversaries, take romantic trips to Europe and take #selfies on the beach. I had to accept that unless I gave up social media for the entire year, I would constantly see things I would not be experiencing anytime soon. And with my business need for event promotion, leaving social media wasn't an option. So I had to learn to deal with it.

I also had to realize that while I was doing my best to fight away the comparisons I made between myself and others, people would soon begin to compare me to others as well. Family friends, church members and people you work with, have no clue why you are single, and yet they feel the need for you to explain to them, "How did this happen to you?" As if it's some disease you caught somewhere along the way. They compare you with other people your age, figuring if Sarah Sue could find a husband and settle down, you definitely could do the same. I'm sure they meant well, but I was on a journey to please God and sometimes that journey isn't one that everyone can understand. So a lot of times I had to simply forgive them in my heart and move on with life.

This higher road was not always easy, especially when comparing yourself to friends who were once single at the same time as you. I remember being around a group of single friends who heard or learned about the one year challenge around the same time as me. There were a few of us who felt led to take it and some that felt their growth during their single season wouldn't require the one year challenge. I honestly believe, that only you could ever personally know if this is a challenge you need to do. However, I would be lying if I wasn't painted with a slight jealousy when soon after I made the commitment to complete the year challenge, some of these single friends started dating. I said to God, seriously, some of these people have been single for four and five years and the minute I say this year is for you, everyone around me starts finding a relationship. This comparison game was killing me. But it was none of my business who took the challenge and who started dating, but in those moments I thought it was.

God then taught me that comparison steals joy. As a human, my heart naturally yearned for the seasons others were experiencing. I soon came to understand the grass isn't always greener on the other side; the grass is greener where you water it. I had to learn to be genuinely happy for my friends. I also had to remind myself that we post/announce the good times of life, not the hard times. So don't envy someone else's portion, when you are only privy to the slide reel of their life that they wanted to show you.

I recently heard a teaching on comparison that also helped to set me free. It was about a man and a group of friends that came into a restaurant, sat down and ordered their food. Fifteen minutes later another group came in and did the same. About thirty minutes later, another group came in and did the same. Eventually, both of those groups that came in after him were given their orders as well as most of the people sitting at his table. Everyone was beginning to get their orders except for him. Confused by this process of service, he called the waitress over to let her know that not only was he the only one at his table that had not received his food, he also watched two separate parties walk into the restaurant after him, and now they too were eating before him as well. He then asked her to explain the problem.

The waitress then explained that what the other people had ordered was a simpler dish and therefore, it took a shorter amount of time to prepare. She told him that he had made a special order, and therefore orders like these usually take a little more time. She then assured him that his order would be there soon. The man's order eventually came, and it was everything he wanted and requested. This teaching was used as a reminder to keep in mind that when you ask God for a special thing, a good thing, and the perfect thing that He set aside for you, it may take a little longer than your neighbor and that's ok. I believe God wants us to be concerned about our portion and not anybody else's dish. God has a timeline for a reason, and we are all on a different timeline according to our purpose. God can grant you anything He wants, whenever He wants, but sometimes we must wait because there is a reason for His timing. We must not grow faint because when it arrives, it will be everything that you prayed for and more.

Sacrifices

In Andy Stanley sermons, he cautioned singles to remain true to their commitment because there will be opportunities to fail. He said, "I want to encourage you to stick to this commitment because in about three months into this challenge you will meet the man or woman of your dreams. You will start to question yourself and then say, well maybe God didn't mean a whole year". Like the rest of the congregation, I laughed at this statement, thinking "Come on if I haven't met anyone during the year and a half before when I was 'technically single,' I definitely wouldn't meet anyone in the next three months." Unfortunately, I was wrong!

Like clockwork, three months into my year challenge, I was sitting in a seminar and the speaker was the living, breathing answer to my exact 'husband list' prayer. He was Single, God-Fearing, Purpose Driven, Family Oriented, Great Job, Personable, Homeowner, No Kids and Scripture quoting kind of a man. "WHAT! No flipping way!!!" I said to myself. If it wasn't bad enough that I was thinking it, my friend kept nudging me on my side during the entire presentation, saying that this has to be the one. I told her no thank you because I was adamant about sticking to my year challenge.

Further, as fate would have it, this guy and I crossed paths again, and a friendship began to form. He became interested in me, and I told him that I had made a commitment to God, and I wasn't able to give up on that commitment. He understood and asked if I would like him to wait until the year was over to date. I told him no because that would defeat the purpose of me taking a 'faith year' from dating. If I was going to be open to whatever God had in store for me, having someone waiting in my back pocket once the year was over would be defeating the purpose. So I respectfully declined his offer to wait. In fact, I even jokingly told him that a friend of mine would make a good catch for him because they were both interested in dating at the time and had similar Christian values.

Now don't get me wrong, although I made this statement to him, I was, for the most part, joking, so I was a little caught off guard by what happened next. That summer when I returned from my "eat, pray, love" vacation, my friend that I jokingly told him about told me she had something to ask me. She told me she ran into the guy this summer at a festival, and they seem to hit off so she wanted to make sure it would be cool with me if she got to know the guy that was my living breathing 'husband list'. Seriously, I thought. She told me they had seemed to get along well, and she thought it could maybe lead somewhere.

This news was a lot to swallow, but having a problem would have been selfish because I hadn't dated the guy. And I wasn't planning to date anyone anytime soon. Who was I to stand in the way, right? I had a whole seven months of a challenge left to go so I gave her my blessing. I would be lying if I didn't say I wasn't a tad bit upset with God. He showed me my list could exist, and then He took it away. That's the thing about God, our plans are not His plans, and I believe He just wanted me to have faith that this kind of man does exist. So if nothing else, meeting this guy did help to restore my faith in that fact.

This connection wasn't *my* beautiful thing, but it led to their beautiful thing. Those two did hit it off and eventually went on to build a life together. In full transparency, in the beginning it was slightly awkward, but when you're trusting God, even during painful moments you know that, "everything works together for good for those who love the Lord and are called according to His purpose" Romans 8:28 (NIV). Believe it or not, I was able to move on and be genuinely happy for this couple.

I was at peace because I knew God was at work. That summer before I had returned from vacation, I asked God to give me a sign. I said, "If this guy is single when my year challenge was over then that means you want me to date him and if he is not that means he's not for me." God sure didn't waste any time answering my prayer, because by the end of the summer God gave me my sign. God assured me that He had begun a great work in me, and I knew He would be faithful enough to complete it. During our walk with God, He will require sacrifices and they're not always sacrifices we want to make. However, He assures us that one day we shall receive our reward. We just have to remember that this reward is promised in Heaven and not necessarily through earthly desires.

Sexual Frustration

Following God isn't about a 'three month rule' or a 'one year rule', 'it's a wait until marriage' rule. When you're not even dating, its scary to think that there is no definite date for when you will be able to enjoy this gift. However, it is still worth the wait. I'm not sure if the days of frustration would be easier if I were a virgin, but I know for sure I would have no idea what I was missing. So if you are a virgin, and you are reading this, if you don't remember anything else I wrote, remember this: SEX BEFORE MARRIAGE IS NOT WORTH IT!! Wait on God; wait for the beauty found in giving your husband or wife the gift that God designed for you to give them. If I could say it a thousand times, I would, please do NOT have sex before you are married because the aftermath of the pain is not worth it.

Now if you are like me and didn't make the choice to remain a virgin, you have probably already had enough sessions with yourself on regret, so I won't add to it. I just sincerely encourage you to accept the renewal of your mind, body, and soul that comes with the gift of celibacy. I will caution you, just because you make up in your mind that you are going to do things God's way, it doesn't mean your body automatically shuts down and makes the commitment to be celibate as well. My mother always cautioned me not to get myself into compromising situations, because your body has no clue that you're not married, and boy was she right. You have to fight constantly, the urges and frustrations that come along with denying your fleshly desires. So the last thing you want to do is put yourself in a compromising position that would tempt you into breaking your vow.

Some people may argue that it's not natural to deny your body in this way. My response is, as a Christian I am required that my flesh die daily. Therefore, I also have to deal with the painful denial of sex until I am married because this is something that God ordained only for marriage. Andy also eloquently addressed this topic in his sermon, stressing the importance of having self-control. He argued that if someone cannot have self-control as a single person, how will this person all of sudden learn to have self-control as a married person? If you can't exercise self-control to remain celibate, how will you resist the urge not to cheat when your husband or wife has to be away for work for six months? How will you remain faithful if your spouse is sick for two years or has to see a therapist for a sexual dysfunction? Would you simply give up on them?

If your answer is no, you will stand by them even though it's hard because you love them, well that's a part of self-control. When you are a Christian, you make a vow as well. I made a vow to be celibate because that's how much I am in love with God, and I don't want to cheat on Him. Being obedient to His Word is hard, but if I desire a relationship with Him, obedience is a part of what I have to do. I want to love God more than I would ever love my husband, so if I don't want to hurt my husband, why would I want to hurt God?

Sex's worst casualties aren't only STD's or unwanted pregnancy. Sex has your soul completely tied and emotionally engrained into the soul of another person long after they have gone on to be with a new person. During that year after and sometimes longer, your soul will cry out a lot of times not just for the physical act but for that emotional tie that you created with that person. God created sex for marriage for a reason. The two unite and will become one. If you are wondering why you can't find the 'one', it's probably because your soul is still longing for the old 'one'. Letting go of this soul tie is exhausting. So you see despite the sexual frustrations of the wait, my soul couldn't afford the risk of getting connected to anyone else because God was already hard at work disconnecting me from my past.

> If you are wondering why you can't find the 'one', it's probably because your soul is still longing for the old 'one'.

Celibacy is not always easy, and I will be the first to admit that my actions and thoughts were not always pleasing to God. Celibacy is not a badge of honor, because when we are truthful we all struggle with impure thoughts, especially during our first year of commitment. I am not perfect, and I'm not asking you to be. I simply want to you to do your best to make and keep a promise to God. I made the promise to God and to my future husband to keep a vow that I know will be worth it in the end. I believe God sees our frustration and is willing to honor our sacrifices. "No cross, no crown."

I know a commitment like this may be hard to start, so below are eight things I do to deal with sexual frustration:

1.   Kneel before the throne and PRAY

2.   Journal my frustrations to God

3.   Exercise

4.   Avoid reading or watching sexually explicit content

5.   Sleep

6.   Avoid compromising situations

7.   Give my accountability partner permission to 'check me'.

8.   Stay busy with healthy activities

Embracing Change

One of the things I had to accept is that my life would never be the same again after this year. Things I used to like to do, people I used to know and goals and dreams I used to have would all have to change. And even though the changes were happening for the better, it wasn't always easy to do. There are times when I slipped back into old traits of being self-centered, needy and possessive, and I had to learn to catch myself!

During the summer of my friend's wedding in Jamaica, she asked, "Do you want me to introduce you to any single guys during the weekend for you to get to know and hang out with while in Jamaica?" Of course when she asked, I immediately said, "NO WAY! I took a year off of dating; I was doing this. I didn't need a 'wedding date'. I could totally go to a destination wedding as a single woman with no date and no potential for one." So she said "Cool, good to know."

Of course, I'm not blind, so when we got to Jamaica, there was a guy that I found cute but I reminded myself of my no dating commitment, so I told myself not to look at him in that way. He would be nothing more than a new friend. We exchanged small talk over the course of the weekend, but it was during the wedding reception that we had an actual conversation. Before I could even get excited about this conversation with this guy, my friend came up to me and said she wanted to introduce him to her cousin. I quickly brushed her off and said, "Sure, sure, go ahead man, I'm good" in the most sarcastic tone ever. I was not good! I know I wasn't dating, but geez I couldn't have a conversation. But I couldn't blame her, apparently he had been asking her about her cousin during the whole weekend and I was more than adamant before the trip that I was 'doing me', so this was not the time for a freak out session.

After the reception, he gave us a ride back to the hotel and there I was sitting in the car steaming. To this day, I still don't even know why I was so upset. When we arrived at the hotel he opened my door and said something, and I quickly brushed it off with a "Yeah, yeah, whatever." What in the world was wrong with me? I didn't even know this guy. Yet, here I was again possessive over someone I didn't even know, "all in my feelings." It took me five minutes after I got out the car before I began laughing at myself. I was so rude to this guy who I barely had a ten-minute conversation with all because I wasn't used to being alone. In the past, I would have insisted on having a 'wedding date' at a destination wedding. Now, God was rewriting my love story and this story required me to learn how to change.

Change can be a very scary thing, but progress can never happen without change. Loneliness, sexual frustration, sacrifices, and comparison are all a part of the growing pains. I'm not afraid to admit my embarrassing situations, moments of weakness and pain because if my testimony helps only one person to get through the rain, my scars would have still been worth it.

Growth Exercise:

1. What growing pains are you still struggling with in your walk with Christ?

2. What are some specific things you can do to overcome the pain?

Chapter 10

Mentors and Accountability Partners

My experience with *The New Rules of Love, Sex, and Dating* would have never happened if I never had a conversation with one of my spiritual mentors. The day I asked him "How did he know his wife was the one?" was the day he helped to change my life. I was struggling with that question, and it was through a mentor that I found the answer. However, at the time I honestly didn't even see him as a mentor, he was just an acquaintance that I would go to now and then for relationship advice. That day I was seeking untainted advice. Therefore, I couldn't ask family members or close friends who may not objectively understand my dilemma, so I took it to someone who could.

Naturally I didn't just want any opinion; I wanted to hear the opinion of a guy who was making his decisions based on Christ's guidance and not his own, so I reached out to Pastor Kyle. The great thing about it is that he never told me what he thought I should do that day. He simply introduced me to a series that would allow God to speak to me in a special kind of way. To this day, I am so grateful for God strategically placing Kyle into my life. He truly helped me to discover my truth. Once we accept Him as our Savior,

God should always have the first and final say over our lives. But I honestly believe that He also places mentors and accountability partners in our path to help guide us along the way.

I believe one of the greatest stories in the Bible on mentorship is the relationship that we see between Naomi and Ruth. Ruth 1:16 (NIV), "But Ruth replied, do not urge me to leave you. Where you go, I will go, and where you stay, I will stay. Your people will be my people and your God my God." Many of us Christian women grew up idolizing the love story of Ruth and how she found her Boaz. However, most people don't realize that Ruth had no clue there was even a Boaz in her future. In fact, when Naomi told her to leave her and go back to her city so that she could remarry, she refused to leave. Naomi stressed that she had lost her husband and her two sons, one being Ruth's husband. She felt bitter and hopeless and urged Ruth to get away from that kind of pain. Naomi wanted Ruth to return to her birth home so that she could find a new husband while she still could.

Ruth decided not to chase after a man when she lost her husband; she chose to chase after Christ. Ruth was more devoted to building a relationship with her mentor than she was to finding a relationship with a new husband. Many of us women have been guilty of crying to God, "Oh God, where is my Boaz?" however, have we ever cried to God and asked, "Where is my Naomi?" Ruth chose to follow the God of Naomi even if it meant that she would be single for the rest of her life. She believed in the guidance of Naomi and knew she could provide a wonderful life for her, even when Naomi didn't believe it herself.

Ruth fought to have a mentor in her life. Even when Naomi tried to send her away, Ruth fought to stay. I wonder how much further we would be as women if we stopped fighting to hold onto the men we want in our lives and started learning to fight

Ruth fought to have a mentor in her life. Even when Naomi tried to send her away, Ruth fought to stay.

for the relationship with an older woman (or man) who has the experience to teach us: women who can teach us how to pray, serve, give, submit, build and flourish within our purpose. I wonder how much further we would be if we adopted Ruth's mentality.

When Naomi realized that Ruth was determined to fight for their relationship, she eventually gave in and started a new life with her in Bethlehem. Ruth's mind was still NOT on finding a husband. Ruth offered to glean the fields to help and provide a better life for her and Naomi. Ruth lived with her mother-in-law for ten years, so I imagine that the teaching she received over those years was the kind of teaching she didn't want to lose. So she showed Naomi her appreciation by staying by her side.

Eventually, Naomi blessed Ruth with the guidance on how to get Boaz to notice her. She listened to the wise counsel of a mentor she trusted and had followed for over ten years. If Ruth hadn't been wise enough to focus on the benefits of mentorship and be patient enough to wait for the guidance of someone older and wiser, she might have never found her Boaz. You see we can't miss the beauty of the book of Ruth by spending so much time in chapter four when she eventually marries Boaz. The true essence of this story crystallizes that happiness happens throughout the journey and not simply at the destination. I found power in learning the importance of mentorship.

Spiritual Mentorship

I had always had a close relationship with my mom growing up, but with your mom there are still certain things you don't feel totally comfortable sharing. This factor is why I often sought out the advice of other spiritual mentors. During my one year challenge, I realized that God had blessed me with a Naomi, who was living with me all along. As I mentioned I hosted my very own *The New Rules of Love, Sex, and Dating* conference during that year and on the last Saturday, we hosted a session where we separated the men and the women for the first hour. In the session with the women, I decided to share my testimony and everything it had taught me in the last few months. Like in this book, I was very transparent about my past, and it was the first time my mother heard me say that I was not a virgin. I am sure it may have crossed her mind a time or two, seeing that it did take me an incredibly long time to let go of any serious relationship I had. But still I had never confirmed it until that day. She never said it, but I'm pretty sure a jolt of disappointment must have graced her heart that day. My mother had saved her gift of virginity until marriage and like any mother, I'm sure she was hoping I would do the same.

My mother confirmed that day why God placed her in my life as not only my mother but as one of my greatest mentors. She didn't judge me, she didn't berate me with dozens of questions about why and she didn't make me feel any more guilty than I already felt on my own. She saw that I had learned from my mistakes and was prepared to move forward, taking my vow of celibacy as important as I wished I had taken the vow of my virginity. I'm sure she felt pain, but instead of punishing me with her words, she simply forgave me. She did, however ask when the workshop was through, if I thought I shared a little too much of my personal life with all of the women who were in the room that day. I laughed to myself because I'm sure being as transparent as I was, can be a little nerve wrecking for anybody. I assured her that I know it may have seemed like a lot, but I only shared what the Holy Spirit gave me clearance to share that day.

Trying to get closer to God can seem like a very foreign thing in the beginning. Therefore having someone to help you navigate this journey is crucial. However you should know that a spiritual mentor doesn't have to be some super religious person with whom you have no common ground. I would suggest someone who is simply committed to grow closer to Christ, someone relatable, open and led by God to helping you along the way.

I remember once crying over a situation to my mom. She had heard this same cry at least fifty times before and this time she said, "Kerel, I'm going to need you to let this go!" I was shocked. She had listened and agreed every time before. But this time agreeing isn't what I needed, I needed the strength of someone wiser to check me and my motives. My relationship with God is where it is today because I realized how important it was to have someone sow into me spiritually along the way.

Mentors in Purpose

Some people have career mentors but I like to also have a purpose mentor. I believe a purpose mentor helps to guide your God-given gifts and talents. I wrote my first short production in 2010. This play was for a playwriting competition that I was so sure that I would win. And although all the odds seem to be in our favor, we still lost. At first I was devastated but then I began to appreciate how much I had learned along the way. The competition assigned each production group a theater mentor and I was matched with Gloria McGlone. Gloria had retired in the Bahamas from the United States after her long career on Broadway in New York. I was amazed at the amount of knowledge she so willingly poured into me as a writer, actor and director. She took our talent to a new level because she made us leave our feelings outside the door and our gifts on the stage. She didn't settle for mediocre and those lessons I learned turned out to be better than any first place finish in a competition.

Years later after I finished writing my first ever full production, there was only one person I wanted to read it – Gloria McGlone. She not only agreed to read it, but she also agreed to be my mentor as I took the journey to making this play come to life. This play was surely a venture I couldn't complete with her guiding hand along the way. Writing has become a part of my purpose, but this talent would have never been sharpened without her patience, talents and wisdom.

In your workplace, it's not about the person who makes the most money, is the most cut throat, nor is it about the person who is your immediate boss. I found that the person most qualified to nurture my gifts and talents was the person willing to teach me, not to gain fortune or fame but simply because she understood that excelling in our purpose is paramount. Purpose mentors help you chase purpose, not paper. So if you are interested in finding someone who would help to sharpen your tools. Seek out someone who is sincere, shares your values and cares about you as a person.

Life Mentor

I once read that if you are the smartest person in the room, then you are in the wrong room. When I finished graduate school the first time, I was placed in a high school as a guidance counselor. Honestly, the first few months weren't that bad. But eventually I began to realize that getting a degree didn't solve the lack of interest that I had in this career as I thought it would. My patience was up, and I needed to get out! However, there turned out to be a long gap between wanting to leave and eventually being able to leave. So after a while the only thing that made me happy to go to work every day was the fact that my office was joined by the open door to one of my favorite persons, Grace!

I once read that if you are the smartest person in the room, then you are in the wrong room.

Grace is still in disbelief when I refer to her as one of my mentors. Although she is only four years older than me, she is filled with the wisdom of an 80-year-old. So she falls into two categories as one of my closest friends and one of my mentors. Grace is a free spirit; I always admired watching her live life with an overwhelming amount of peace.

When I began working at the high school I was in a serious relationship and Grace was single. Despite being four years older than me, she was still in no rush to be a wife. In fact, she never even talked about it. She would take summer trips to Canada and daydream about future trips to Europe and the Maldives. Grace is one of the few black girls I know that would swim two hours before she heads to work, come home, blow dry her hair and walk in with perfect bouncing hair and a big smile on her face. She played in a band and was the one soul that all the teachers came to talk to about their issues. We were there for the students, but it seemed like almost every teacher and support staff gravitated towards her awesome energy. She took in the beauty of reading great novels and appreciated the simplicity and joy found in great food and a great glass of wine. And on top of all of that, she is one the smartest women I know.

As someone who was crazy over relationships and my life goals in general, Grace served as a constant reminder that being single was a time to enjoy life, discover new things and simply be happy. She also helped to heighten my appreciation for the finer things in life, while providing a listening ear as I went through my various ups and downs. Grace trusted God's timing and His plans for her life and that was a place I wanted to be. Ironically, Grace got married during my one year challenge. I was now single and she had found herself in the place I had always dreamed of being. And she got there without ever once obsessing about being married. One day she fell in love and eventually everything else just began to fall into place. Grace's story served as a reminder to me that just because God sees you enjoying your life as a single person, it doesn't mean He says, "Cool, I'll move on and bless someone else, since you are so content in being single." It simply means you have learned that His word is true; that everything is beautiful in its time. When you have the opportunity to find a mentor/friend whose life is living example of trusting God's will, you have truly found a good thing.

During this year, I asked myself, "Who are you allowing to sow into your life, to speak over your life and to influence you?" I strongly encourage having a mentor that knows you personally and can have a close relationship with you. And also that you can allow someone to speak into your life as a mentor by just reading their books, watching their interviews and following their social media. Heather Lindsey, T.D. Jakes, Kim Pothier, Toure Roberts, Sarah Jakes - Roberts, Steve Harvey, Ashley and Carrington Brown, have all had testimonies and daily encouragement that have helped to change my life. When we place ego aside and see the beauty of a mentor, our life will begin to change.

Mentees

I believe it's also important for us to put the shoe on the other foot and also seek to be a blessing to the Ruth's in our lives. When you have someone who you know looks up to you, it challenges you to be conscious of your actions. I competed in my last pageant in 2011 and officially became a pageant interview coach in 2012. I continually coached and mentored girls voluntarily because, for me, my reward wasn't in a monetary donation; it's in the transformation I got to see in these beautiful women. People constantly called me crazy for giving away so much of my time for free, but none of that mattered to me, because I got the opportunity to help women explore who they were meant to be. My favorite part of any pageant is the interview round. In an interview, a judge urges a contestant to tell them who they are, their goals, values, opinions, hopes, and dreams. For most women, this is the first time they are forced to take an introspective look at how they define themselves. And in a society where so many people lack genuine self-awareness, it brings me great joy to help these women to dig deep into their truth.

My sorority's organization The Twenty Pearls program also provided me with the gift of mentorship when I had the opportunity to have a constant interaction with a group of the most intelligent and purpose driven high school girls I have ever met. Usually when you enter mentorship, it's with the sole purpose to be a blessing in someone else's life but the inspiration I gained from their hopeful faces every week was just as priceless. Those two and half years I spent leading and pouring into those girls are years I will never forget. Your mentee may be a godchild, family member, or a part of a community group. No matter where he or she is in your life, God didn't bless you with all of that wisdom and experience for you to simply keep it to yourself. You may be surprised by the amount of growth you pursue yourself when you realize someone else is watching and waiting to be led by you.

Accountability Partners

I remember begging God at the beginning of my one year challenge to send me women on a similar journey as me, women that could be a support system through this journey. I love the fact that a mentor can tell you that they know it's hard, and they know that you will make it through. There is peace in knowing that there was a time when they were single and honestly trusted God to answer their prayers and He did. This makes you believe that if He did it for them, He can do it for you. This line always reassures my faith and at that moment I know God hasn't forgotten about me. But to be honest there are days I just want to vent to someone who knows exactly how I'm feeling right now.

Some days I honestly want to scream at those married women I follow on social media and say: "You don't know my struggle! Yeah, you've been through it before, but you're not going through it now. When I cry at night, you're snuggling with your husband, it's easy for you to share your struggles about back then, because you're not there now, but who's going to relate to what I'm struggling with now?" So if you ever had one of those days, I encourage you to use those days to turn to the "David's" or "Jonathan's" in your life. For those who may not know the story, when I refer to David and Jonathan, I'm not talking about potential romantic relationships, but those platonic relationships with other singles that are on this journey with you.

David and Jonathan's friendship is one of the most well-known friendships in the Bible. David was set to become King after Saul and eventually he joined Saul's family by marrying Jonathan's sister. 1 Samuel 18:3 (NIV), "And Jonathan made a covenant with David because he loved him as himself. Jonathan took off the robe he was wearing and gave it to David, along with his tunic and even his sword, his bow, and his belt." Things began to go south when Saul became jealous of David and tried to kill him. Jonathan protected David; he didn't side with his father and in the effort to save the life of his friend, eventually Jonathan ended up losing his life. Your accountability partner is the kind of friend that will go to great lengths to protect you. They'll encourage you, challenge you and stand in the gap for you. When you walk on a journey towards your higher calling, there will be days where you feel attacked emotionally, spiritually and maybe even physically. Therefore I urge you, to make sure the person feeding you, is full of a David or Jonathan spirit.

Accountability partners support you in your journey to get closer to Christ. They are the ones who will be that listening ear you vent to when you have a frustrating day. This kind of friend will quickly volunteer to hand out programs at your event because they realized you forgot to assign someone to do it. A supportive friend will help to be your pillar of strength when you forget why you started this journey in the first place. Supporting your decision to no longer frequent the nightclub, get drunk or entertain random guys. They want to see you thrive in the things God has called you to do.

I am thankful that God not only sent me a supportive friend that I grew closer to that year, but she also started her one year challenge just a few months after me. My accountability partner was also yearning for a deeper relationship with Christ. She understood the triumphs and struggles of my current season, and it made the journey just a little easier because I know I wasn't walking it alone.

Thomas Edison encouraged Mr. Ford to believe in his dreams, so who are you encouraging?

Accountability partners understand your vision. I have been blogging for over two years now, and I still light up like a little child when a friend or acquaintance tells me, "I read your blog today, and it truly blessed me."

Before this book, my blog was the only outlet I used to express myself on a regular basis. Every time I questioned if I was sharing a little too much or wondering if a topic was timely enough, God sent someone who left an email, inbox message or text saying, "Thank you, you have no idea how much I needed to hear that word today." Those were the days that I knew my writing wasn't in vain. It was because of those individuals that I had the courage to write my first book. Their encouragement and just simple support brought me the greatest joy. Maybe you exercise your interest in a different way, whether it's through music, dance or your recommendation of really great books. No matter what it is, when you have a friend that simply 'gets you' it provides reassurance that your process of growth isn't in vain. Like the characters, Meredith Grey and Christina Yang from *Grey's Anatomy*, we all need our person.

Accountability partners are also purpose driven. I once sat in a seminar that asked you to check the board of directors in your life. Who is sitting at your table? Thomas Edison encouraged Mr. Ford to believe in his dreams, so who are you encouraging? And who's encouraging you? I think it's crucial to your growth to surround yourself with people that are as purpose driven as you.

It doesn't matter what career you are pursuing, I am more concerned about your intent and motives behind the things you pursue. If you want to be a writer to write trashy novels because they sell and you just want to find a way to make a lot of money, then you're not someone that I want at my table. However, if you are a writer who wants to write a variety of things but at the end of the day you want to know that in some way you have encouraged, inspired or motivated someone to be a better person, then you're the kind of person I need on my team.

The minute you ask God to bring these kinds of people into your life you will begin to see friendships formed. I remember being asked to do the exhausting task of being the Mistress of Ceremonies at an all-day conference for over 100 teenage girls. I had to be a ball of energy that day as I kept them entertained and kept the schedule rolling throughout the day. That day I met someone who became another 'Jonathan' in my life.

One of the speakers during that day was around the same age as me and during one of the breaks we began to have a conversation about who we were and things we were both doing in the community. We decided to keep in contact and the next time she was hosting her very own conference she invited me to be the Mistress of Ceremonies. After this, our friendship continued to grow tremendously. We are not the kind of friends who talk every day but as purpose driven women we see the value of surrounding ourselves with someone who is on the same journey that we are. We support each other's events, bounce ideas off each other and attend conferences together. Having an accountability partner who is moving towards the same goal of growth as you, pushes you to continue to be bold enough to conquer what God has called you to do.

Finally, accountability partners are honest and direct with you; they don't sugarcoat the truth. These friends will push you to check your motives and question ideas you have, that may seem a bit off. Though I have many of these kinds of friends, my two best friends from college share the bulk of this role in my life equally. When you know someone is going to question your behavior it serves as God's reminder in human form. They may say I need you to evaluate what you have done or about to do because it doesn't line up with your beliefs. I don't believe in surrounding myself with 'yes' people because I won't grow if I don't have persons bold enough to challenge me. We all have blind spots so we can't let ourselves become too sensitive or insecure about having someone on our team that is strong enough to tell us the truth.

I once read somewhere that "We don't want people in our lives that will help us grow we want people in our lives who will make us feel good." As I said before, growth to me is everything, so if you're not going to help me grow, then you will have to go! No man is an island and if it weren't for my mentors and accountability partners, completing my year challenge would have been impossible. If you struggle with the above questions, pray and ask God to identify or help you find a Mentor, Mentee, and Accountability partner to help you grow.

Growth Exercise:

1. Who are the key mentors in your life and how do they add to you spiritually and purposely?

2. Who are the mentees in your life and how do you add value to their life?

3. Who are the key accountability partners in your life and how are you pushing each other towards Christ?

Chapter 11
The Wait

The last few months of my one year challenge, I began to get involved in our local theater, and I was beginning to see signs of my purpose take form. As the countdown to January 30th, 2014 began, I was excited. I had done it! Christ was there through the hard times, and I was ready for 2014 to be my year of harvest. However, there was one problem; my Father in heaven did not synchronize the end of my one year challenge with a new romantic relationship. A relationship wasn't the promise in the sermon, but naturally I was hoping it would happen. So I did the unthinkable; I flew up in God's face as if my 'works' were worthy of a reward. I wanted my fruit after twelve months of 'sacrifice'. I felt duped. Weeks went by without a glimmer of hope, and I began to enter the aftermath.

It had been 22 days since my year challenge ended, and I was angry at God. I believe God sometimes closes the doors you desperately want open on purpose and sometimes that purpose doesn't play out exactly how we expected. Imagine this: for an entire year you force yourself to disconnect from all romantic relationships in efforts to restore your love for God and learn to love yourself, yet God still says you aren't ready.

This season is where I learned that God is not a genie. I was humbled and told that I could not earn my gifts and rewards. God told me, you don't deserve a man because you

> You will be presented with a partner in purpose only when you are truly ready and not one moment before.

sacrificed twelve months. You will be presented with a partner in purpose only when you are truly ready and not one moment before. I realized that being upset and angry at God during the aftermath was a plan of the enemy to show God that I didn't take the year off to get to know Him, love Him and surrender to who He created me to be. I took the year off as a bargaining chip to try and persuade God to bring my husband much sooner. "God, I won't date anyone for a whole year, but at the end of that year my husband is going to have to be waiting on that doorstep for me." That wasn't the prayer that left my lips, but it was the prayer that I realized I deceitfully held in my heart.

I thought God completely stripped me during my ONE year of sacrifice, but if God was still making me wait, although it was painful, I knew it was for a good reason. I know there may be some other people reading this book who may say, "Well that's all well and good and maybe you gave God a year but I gave God 5, 8 or 10 years, why I am still here?" Well, I wrote this chapter to encourage you as well.

If you enter into this season of waiting, do not faint; it just means that the blessing God has in your life requires you to go through a longer developmental stage. I took 27 years of bad habits and prayed they would all go away in one year, but it just doesn't work that way. God wanted me to be fully prepared for marriage because He knew that new levels bring new devils. God is not surprised about where we are; He knew we would be lonely, He knew we would be frustrated and anxious. But Christ has promised if we don't give up the fight it will be worth the wait.

Now although this sounds all well and good, like a lot of people I hate waiting and I will be the first to admit that patience was never really a strong point for me. Over the years, I learned if you spend your time doing nothing while you are waiting, you will begin to frustrate yourself. Some of us have learned to master staying busy during a waiting process. During my one year challenge, I didn't mind waiting because I was making a conscious decision, not to date. However, once my one year challenge was complete, waiting became ten times harder.

We play this same theory out when we travel. We will find a million things to do during our five-hour layover in the airport by surfing the internet, reading, watching a movie or catching a quick nap. However, the minute our ride from the airport is even ten minutes late picking us up, we're ready to blow a fuse. The difference between the two of these scenarios is our expectations. I can't imagine the riot act we would give to someone who came an entire five hours late to pick us up from the airport, which would be simply unacceptable right? Some people may even say that this is a pretty fair expectation to have, but what happens when we start putting these kinds of expectations on God? I expected God to have my husband ready and waiting once my one year challenge was complete. I had arrived at the end of the finish line, and he was supposed to be there to pick me up right? But God doesn't always work that way.

As I travel now, I have learned to be prepared to take out my book to read during my five-hour layover and as I wait to be picked up from the airport. This has made me less irritable when the person doing me a favor arrives late. As a frequent traveler, my ride may not always be there on time, but they always arrive. It's important for us to stop placing expectations on God to meet our needs when we want him to and be open to staying busy with Him until he decides to bless us with a new season. "God may not come when you want him, but he's always on time!"

Motives

James 4:3 (NIV) says, "When you ask, you do not receive because you ask with the wrong motives that you may spend what you get on your pleasures." I think one of the reasons God keeps us waiting is because He wants us to genuinely check our motives. Are we asking for a life of marriage for the wrong reasons? I remember after I finished my one year challenge I had a mentor ask me, "Why do you want to get married so bad?" I was kind of shocked at her question. I thought it was obvious, but I obliged and answered, "Well I want to be able to have someone to share life with, to talk to and rub my feet at night. I want to have someone to have children with and be able to build a family together." I sat there very proud of my answer because wasn't this the reason everyone wanted to get married? Marriage is the answer to a lifetime companionship, and a Christ led family that we all want.

Then she asked what would I do if my husband worked a very intensive job that kept him from coming home early every night, coupled with the fact that I wasn't physically able to have any children and your husband then refused adoption, would you still want to be married? She stripped my motives for marriage to threads, and I sat with the painful reality that I wanted to get married for me. I wanted my husband to meet my needs and, of course, I would meet his, but I wasn't considering meeting the needs of Christ. At that moment, I silently thanked all my previous boyfriends who didn't give in to marrying me. I wasn't ready and yes maybe I would have figured it all out, but what if I didn't? God hid me because He knew my motives for marriage weren't pure. Although my year challenge was over, God still had some things for me to do, and one of those things was to check my motives.

I believe God blessed me with unique abilities to draw others to Him. So therefore my marriage should be an extension of that. I had to learn that marriage, just like my life, is a ministry. It's not just about having babies and companionship it's about sharing a life with someone that is on the same journey as me. God checked my motives and asked if I wanted to get married to please myself and fulfill society's standards of marriage or did I want a marriage that pleased Him. Talk is cheap, but God knows our heart.

Assignments

Sometimes I think God also makes us wait because we have unfinished assignments that He wants us to complete. I got the call from God to begin this book, 22 days after my year challenge was complete. However, I didn't put pen to paper until almost an entire year later. This scenario reminds me of the book of Haggai. In this book, God sent Haggai to tell his people that the time had come for them to rebuild the house of the Lord. Haggai 1:6 (NIV), "You have played much, but you have harvested little. You eat but never have enough. You drink but never have your fill..." God told His people that they expected much but received little because they decided to finish their houses instead of focusing on the house of the Lord. We are often very guilty of the same things; we focus and place our energy and efforts on the things that we want, instead of the things that will bring honor and glory to God. Then we cry and ask God why He hasn't blessed us with the things we want. As the people of Judah, God is waiting for us to finish His assignments. What has God instructed you to do, that you have constantly been putting on hold?

Everyone's assignment is different. For you maybe it's starting a new business, traveling the world, starting or completing your graduate degree or maybe even buying a home. Sometimes we think if we sit down and 'pout' out our mouths, instead of enjoying the life we have been given, maybe God will feel sorry for us and answer our call. However, God cannot be manipulated. He has given us assignments for a reason, and the Lord says when we are faithful to Him, He will abide in us.

I have a friend who was a 32-year-old, single working woman that decided it was time to buy a home. After settling in her career, she decided this was the next move God wanted her to make. Although she felt confident in her decision, many people still frowned on this independent move. Thinking that it sends the message that I have given up on buying a home with my future husband, and now I'm settling for a future on my own. But, single women or men who buy a house as a single person are simply strong enough to say if I have someone to share this house with one day, great, and if not I have come to realize that I still have a pretty great life ahead of me. So with this spirit, she bought the house.

Shortly after buying the house she went out shopping for furniture and different knick-knacks. It was in the store while searching for new appliances that she met her future husband. **Sometimes our blessings are waiting on the opposite side of our obedience.** If God is telling you to do something, no matter how crazy it sounds to everyone else or even you, you have to be willing to move. You have to be willing to begin and complete your assignment. Stop asking the question "Where is my Adam?" and start asking the question "God what is it that you have called me to do in this season?"

Pass Some Tests

After taking a year off, I think God also wanted to know if I was ready for this next season. Whenever we complete a certain level of our education, even if it's just one class, there is usually a test at the end. This waiting period a lot of times felt like a testing period. God wanted to know if I was able to keep my eyes on Him and His faithfulness. He used the test to reveal to me that despite my time away from dating, there was still work to do; my eyes were on marriage. When I evaluated my conversations, places I frequented and daily desires, my heart was not set on Christ. God would place me in situations to choose His will over mine and every time I chose mine. It was a reminder to Christ that I was not ready for the next season. This time with God reminded me of the phrase, "Sometimes God doesn't change your situation because He is desperately trying to change your heart."

I will admit that sometimes instead of praying about a situation I would run ahead of God. I told God this time of waiting had been entirely too long, so He must be able to bless a relationship with one of the people. How many times do we get ourselves in situations and then ask God to place His stamp of approval on it? Yet, God's call has been so deep in my life, He has made it almost impossible for me to ignore the lack of peace I have when things are simply not right. I had to realize that these 'potentials' were carbon copies of what God has in store for me and settling wasn't an option. I believe God allows temptations to test your growth and to check your motives.

When that older family member asks why you are taking so long to get married, that's God testing your patience. When your best friend gets engaged, and you still don't have a potential, that's God testing your faith in His timing. When you watch your ex-boyfriend or ex-girlfriend move on in life with someone new, remember that's God testing your understanding of His will prevailing over your own. God never said living a life for Him would be easy; He just promised you it would be worth it.

We sit amazed at the great stories of the Bible, that featured great men like Noah, David, Abraham and Joseph, but we often forget that they also went through a season of waiting before they ever experienced their reward. Noah's ark took 120 years to build. That was 120 years of people calling him crazy, foolish and delusional, but he had a promise from God. David waited 15 years to become king and most of those years were spent running for his life, from the hand of his father-in-law. Can you imagine being told you would be king 15 years before you became one? Abraham was 100 years old before he was able to have a son, and Joseph spent 13 years in Potiphar's house. He was also in prison for two of those 13 years, all before God rewarded him as Governor and gave him a wife. If God is making you wait, you are in great company, because God always fulfill his promises.

Contentment

Whatever state you find yourself be content. I remember the first time I participated in a beauty pageant. I lost over 50 pounds, I started to volunteer more in my community, and I went to pageant practices three to four times a week for five months and at the end of all of that hard work I received an instant reward. On February 3rd, 2008, I won the first pageant that I had ever entered; I felt the joy that came when hard work paid off. The excitement I felt was electric. Anyone who has ever won something after wanting it for so long knows the adrenaline and contentment of having your dream come true. My dream came true that day.

The next phase was to go on to the national level to compete for Miss Bahamas. So again I began to work with my trainer, attend weekly pageant practices and got into the mind frame of another competition. During this time in my life, life really couldn't be better. I was living my dreams through pageantry, I was in a steady and loving relationship, and I was enjoying the benefits of a free travel schedule, I was on cloud nine.

When it came down to final pageant weekend, after looking at the competition, I felt that I at least had the chance of gracing the Top Three. That night I didn't even make the Top Five. Needless to say, I was devastated. Twenty-four hours before this, I was on top of the world, but after only being called for the Top Ten, I felt like I had the wind knocked out of me. For days my boyfriend, friends, and family tried to comfort me and remind me of all the great things I still had going on. However, it took 'forever' for me to find contentment. I could not shake this depression, until one day someone reminded me that I was still a local pageant title holder. I didn't lose anything that I didn't already have in my life four months ago, when I was sitting on top of the world. So how could I be so devastated and unappreciative when four months ago before I ever won my first pageant, I was praying for everything that I currently had?

In life, we sometimes become so tunneled vision on a certain job post, a child, an acceptance letter or marriage, that we forget that we are currently in the midst of a million answered prayers.

If we don't learn to be content with our current state, there will always be something else we desire.

At the end of my one year challenge, I was pursuing my second Master's degree, I had finished writing my first full production play and I was finally at peace with my purpose. My relationship with Christ was where I always wanted it to be, I had found me. However, not having a spouse forced me not to be content. If we don't learn to be content with our current state, there will always be something else we desire. After the wedding vows, our contentment would be wrapped up in establishing a successful life together, and then it will be wrapped up in a child, and then in the pursuit of another child and the vicious cycle of wants and desires will spiral because nothing can fill the void of discontentment like Christ.

So, I didn't want to simply say I was content with Christ, I wanted it to be genuine, and I wanted to believe it. I apologize in advance because yes, there has been once or twice that I have posted a message of encouragement about waiting for God's best. Yet those women and even sometimes men, who post a message every day about how content they are waiting on God or how they know their spouse is on the way can sometimes irritate me. I'm sorry, but a constant daily message about your "contentment" as a single in waiting makes me think, "Thou does protest too much."

Why can't we just be happy that we ran seven miles today, and that's it? Not "I ran seven miles today alone, but that's ok because I will soon run seven miles with my husband to be and then I will be as happy as can be. #wifetobe #acouplethatworksouttogether #staystogether". Sometimes I just want to scream, "No! You're not in that season yet, so stop consistently talking about it". Now I can't tell you what to do, and this is just my opinion. And honestly I think a little self-encouragement now and then is fine. However, I think a constant obsession with "waiting" stifles growth. I think we will be able to be content in a season when we take our minds off of the thing we are waiting for and learn to simply enjoy what's currently in front of us.

In efforts to do just this and have a dose of my own medicine, I took this past summer to do the 100 Happy Day Challenge, and it was so worth it. The 100 Happy Day Challenge is designed to make people more positive, grateful and at times, channel new and amazing opportunities into their life. The 100 Happy Day Challenge is kind of simple; first you choose a form of social media to post on: Facebook, Twitter, Instagram or Email. (I chose Instagram), and then every day for 100 Days in a row, just post a picture of something that made you happy that day or makes you happy in general. It could be anything from lunch with a good friend, a good book or even a quote that brightened up your day. Then Hash Tag #100Happydaychallenge and then create your own hash tag like #enjoythejourneykp so that you can keep track of the 100 Days you reflected on being happy. The Challenge website states 71% of people never complete this challenge claiming they had no time to keep up with it. I am so glad I did it because this was honestly one of the best summers I ever had. So the question is: Do you have the time to be happy?

There were a lot of happy days during my challenge, but there were also a lot of hard days. Days when I couldn't find anything to be happy about and days when I simply didn't want to be happy. Still, every day that passed without any foreseen goal at the end, I consistently found something to make me happy. No one promised me there would be some great reward at the end of it all; I just knew finding a way to be happy no matter what was bound to make my life more fulfilling. I don't know what your future holds, but I want to remind you that wherever you are going, it's not about the destination. We don't know what God has planned for us, but he wants us to be content. God wants us to enjoy the journey along the way, and if we have faith in Him, He will be faithful enough to blow our minds. "Let us not become weary in doing good, for at the proper time we will reap a harvest if we do not give up." Galatians 6:9

Grace

When you understand the grace of God, you learn to accept that His timing is perfect. God has saved me from so many unfortunate circumstances and situations in my dating life. It was only His grace that could have brought me through. We can't look at friends or counterparts and sadly complain that she or he has only been single for two weeks and I have been single for two years and then ask where is my happy ending? We have to realize that we are not on the same path as our neighbor. Comparison is the thief of joy, and everyone's story is going to be different.

The reason we get so fed up when we feel like someone who has done less for God is getting blessed before we are, is because we think we can earn God's love. God's not counting your two years of sacrifice as some bargaining chip. Yes, there are things God has called us to do, but they aren't so that we can 'earn' His love or favor, just that we can simply love and serve Him. We sin every day, so no matter how hard we try we could never earn God's favor. God's gift of grace is the gift that is free.

So when you tell God it's not fair that you gave someone else a spouse and didn't give me one, you are insulting God's gift of grace to you. God's grace may have saved you from an abusive spouse, a loveless marriage, extramarital affairs, unwanted pregnancies, sexually transmitted diseases or financial burdens. We don't realize that sometimes we are banging on the door that God was gracious enough to shut. Your season of singleness is a gift. It may be a gift that a lot of us may not want, but it is a gift that we desperately need. Understanding and prospering in a season of singleness will only make us more equipped to handle the gift of marriage.

So don't despise this season, because there is someone dying for the life that you are currently living. The sad thing is when we take our eyes off of what we have in front of us and focus on the wait, we forget about the days when we prayed for the things that we currently have. We cannot forget that we didn't earn our current blessings. Your great job, new home, expendable income and new car were all given to you as a gift of grace from God. So the next time you begin to question, why after all that you have done, God still has you in a season of waiting, remember God's grace is sufficient unto you. God is never wrong, and His timing is never late. Stay faithful!

Growth Exercise:

1. List three things God has blessed you with in the past after a long wait?

2. Pray and ask God what is it he is still waiting for you to do during your waiting season?

RESTORATION

Chapter 12
Finding Your Purpose

After accepting my time alone, I could probably think of a dozen reasons why God still had me waiting. However, one of the main reasons that kept replaying in my mind was PURPOSE. During the year challenge, I began to discover my purpose, but I still wasn't where God needed me to be when I meet my spouse. He showed me no matter how hard you try to escape it; your purpose will run after you.

In my early twenties, all I could think about was having that 9 to 5 or better yet a 9 to 3, two children, a white picket fence and a dog. However, a part of me believes I would have sat in my house feeling incomplete if this actually became my reality. Even though I believe my children and husband would have brought me a great sense of joy, I know deep within my heart there would've still been a void. Despite the 9 to 3 schedule, I hated my job as a guidance counselor. I felt unfulfilled and used every opportunity during summers and after school to do things that I love. So many people asked how in the world you stayed on a job for 8 ½ years if you hated it. Well, that was easy. It was the 'perfect family job'.

You see, I didn't grow up dreaming about chasing my God-given purpose; I grew up dreaming about a family. So fighting to hold onto my relationships and heading to a job I hated every day was

If I had taken the opportunity to find myself, I would have learned to pursue purpose and not people.

how I thought I was going to reach my 'happy ending'. I once heard a wise Bahamian professor once say, "We must stop teaching our little girls to wait for the day when Prince Charming finally finds them and start teaching them about how to find themselves." If I had taken the opportunity to find myself, I would have learned to pursue purpose and not people.

Eventually, I realized that my constant begging and pleading for the life I wanted would not prevail, and I decided to chase purpose. I took some time to myself to hear God's voice, direction and development of my purpose. God told me: "Allow me to complete you, so you can fully walk into the purpose I have for you." It was during the summer of my one year challenge while sitting in my sister's apartment in North Carolina that I began to live out my purpose. As I mentioned, my dreams had been dashed in a playwriting competition years before. So taking on a project of this magnitude was a bit overwhelming, I questioned my talent, my skill and my ability to make people laugh, however, the thoughts were all there, so I began to let them flow.

Without even knowing it, writing became a therapeutic process for me. I gave life to characters through my pain. There was no main character that completely resembled my life; however they all had a piece of me within their DNA. I wrote about heartbreak, insecurity, deceit, betrayal, forgiveness, self-awareness and love. The scenarios may have been different from what I was personally going through, but the themes ran straight from my soul. Without even knowing it, God was using my passionate heart to touch the lives of others.

When I began my play, I had no idea how I would get people to see it. I had a vision of what I thought it could be, but the how, with who and all of the logistics that had to occur in the between, had me drawing a blank. So I decided to sit on my script and simply wait in faith. The funny thing about God is He will never give you a promise that you are not able to sustain. Six months after sitting on my play, my preparation had finally met an opportunity.

Success Happens
When Preparation Meets Opportunity

I have often heard the phrase that we are only able to control two things: how we prepare for a moment, and how we respond to a moment. However what exactly happens in a moment is all left up to God. Sitting in a meeting for the Freeport Player's Guild's "YARD" (Young Adult Regency Drama) group, my dream began to come alive. YARD being a fairly new group to the theater was looking for a play to launch their reputation in the community, and I wanted the opportunity to share my voice. I pitched my play to the board, and when there were no other viable options, I got the job! I could have spent the previous six months beating the pavement looking for avenues to grow my seed, but sometimes God just wants us to wait in silence for our moment and my moment was here!

The Freeport Player's Guild had been a staple in the Grand Bahama community for many years, with a great reputation for providing Community Theater to the city of Freeport. The involvement in the Freeport Player's Guild is on a complete volunteer basis. Therefore, I entered into this agreement with the sole purpose of spreading the powerful messages of forgiveness. There was no money involved, but that was alright with me. I wanted to tell a story with flawed individuals; I wanted the audience to realize that no matter how much we mess up in life, we are still a character worth rooting for. Subconsciously I believe I was simply trying to find a way to forgive myself.

In late January of that year, my show was sent to the Bahamas Theater Board for approval. In retrospect, I understand why at the end of my year challenge, during that January, why God didn't introduce me to my husband. He had just gotten me into the swing of my purpose and was not about to let me get distracted now. So by March of 2014, the first auditions were held. With an intense six weeks of rehearsals and a cast of over 24 young people all under the age of thirty, we began to put in the work.

I remember the day when it all began to become real to me, it was April 6, 2014, my 29th birthday, and my words were no longer just on a page, they were staring right in front me. We were shooting the promo photos and videos for the show and for the first time I saw my characters come alive. The photographer then began to ask me to tell him the story lines so that he could capture the true essence of the play in his photos. As I spit out various scenarios, he desperately tried to keep up with all of the scandals, and twist and turns of these four friends. He then looked at me, smiled and said "Oh this is going to be good!" Other than the nod I received from my mentors who completed the first proofreads for me, this was the first feedback I received from an outsider on my play. He hadn't even read the script or even seen it yet, but with just the gist of my slide reel, he confirmed everything that I was hoping. My play had the potential to be a success!

We hit the ground hard with promotions and after much anticipation; we finally graced the stage of the Regency Theater in the debut performance of *Sarah's Wedding*. With about 100 people in attendance, the cast was greeted at the end of their Gala performance with a standing ovation. To a lot of people, a 100 people may seem like a small number, but for a first-time playwright, I was on cloud nine again. No one had ever seen my work and on a Gala night everyone who came was willing to pay double the price. So if we had fifty people, I would have been excited. I kept replaying the story of Tyler Perry in my mind. For six years, he rewrote the same play and every year, used all his savings to perform to a room of thirty people. So the gratitude I felt for those 100 people who took a chance on me, was unexplainable.

Their attendance for me was enough, so what happened next was a complete surprise. I got home to see my Facebook newsfeed filled with countless reviews. Those 100 people went home and sold my show. It was surreal that a few months ago, I was dealing with agony and despair and right before my eyes, I had turned my pain into purpose. The reviews from this audience left every other night of *Sarah's Wedding* with a completely sold out show. *Sarah's Wedding* was then requested to be brought back by popular demand, not just once but twice, earning nearly $20,000 in profit from a total of five performances and as promised all of these funds were donated back to keeping Community Theater alive in Grand Bahama.

Leap of Faith

The play then began to receive rave reviews not only on the island of Grand Bahama but also across the Bahamas through various forms of social media. Residents in Nassau, Abaco, and even Exuma all wanted to know about *Sarah's Wedding*. Therefore after much prayer and consultation from veterans in the business, I took a leap of faith and independently sought to bring *Sarah's Wedding* to the capital of the Bahamas, Nassau. This venture didn't prove to be an easy task, and the board that approved my show in Grand Bahama didn't feel comfortable with me taking the show on the road independently. My previous venture had a very low-risk rate because the board had funded and profited from the production. The biggest costs would have been the rental of the actual theater, a theater that was owned by the board, so essentially there was no major cost the first time I put up the show.

However taking the show on the road would have meant plane tickets, housing, transportation, theater rental and a whole new slate of marketing and advertising all for a cast and crew of almost thirty people. After praying about it, I felt that this was a leap of faith God wanted me to take on my own. It was extremely scary showing up on another island with a $1,000 and a dream, but God was ready to show me just how big He was.

I spent six weeks away from home, in Nassau, on the ground gathering support for the show, and this proved to be quite overwhelming. I had a whole team and an entire board with me at home. Now, until my cast arrived a few days before show time, I was flying this plane solo. The only way I was able to make it through that journey was God. My stress level was high; I felt like a fish out of the water, and I was just praying that even though we were in a new city, that the people would still come. I remember borrowing a friend's car to do on the road promotions and after receiving the run around for the third time with the government agency responsible for putting up my Billboards, her car stopped. I couldn't believe it, I was fresh out of savings, had no clue how I would pay for plane tickets of a cast of 28 that was traveling in a few days and just like that the car stopped. At that moment, I began to cry out to God, "How come this was so hard?" My tears wouldn't stop flowing, and I was beginning to question if I had made a big mistake!

At that moment, God revealed that it was hard because He didn't want me to forget that I couldn't do this without Him. After a few minutes of prayer and a whole lot of tears, the car started again, and I was on my way. The minute I got any money from ticket sales in my hand I began to pay off another bill. However, the obstacles kept coming. At four p.m. on the day of the show, I was still looking for intricate pieces of my stage's set but God decided to show up. By eight p.m. that night we had everything we needed, the lights went up and we performed to a full house. Matthew 9:29 (NIV), "According to your faith, let it be done unto you."

Taking my show on the road was one of the most challenging, nerve wracking and stressful ventures I had ever faced. However, if asked if I would do it all over again, the answer would be yes, a thousand times YES! My cast got an all-expenses paid trip to another island, stayed in a three-story beach house and performed every night to a full house. A total of close to 1,200 people came to see them perform that weekend. The smiles on their face after that experience made my extreme exhaustion all worth it.

Throughout the next year, *Sarah's Wedding* received various accolades and awards: the *Freeport Player's Guild Award for Overall Best Production* and a national recognition when I was nominated for the Bahamian Icon Award in Entertainment. I had truly turned a painful experience into purpose. I learned in this process that experience is not just what happens to you, it's what you do with what happens to you.

The Courage to Dream Again

My *Sarah's Wedding* experience opened my eyes to countless new opportunities. I started to dream about making the play into a movie. I now dream of not just making one movie but making several movies: writing TV shows, books, and internationally acclaimed plays, I started to dream about them all. I began to describe myself as a small island girl with big city dreams and even though I have yet to see these dreams come to pass, I have faith that one day they will. Being from a small chain of islands in the Bahamas makes many people feel that Hollywood or even international dreams are impossible. But I like to say, if your dream doesn't scare you, you're not dreaming big enough.

Tyler Perry had a dream and after six years of 'failure', I'm pretty sure he thought his dream was pointless as well. Still, he didn't give up, you want to know why? It wasn't just an interest or a hobby for him; he was chasing his purpose. He says that no matter how many times he experienced failure, he always believed that it would work. In 1998, he decided this was going to be his last show, and if it didn't work, he would give up. That night his show was completely sold out. I believe that when we give up trying to do it on our own, that is when we give God permission to step in. Tyler Perry is now a multi-millionaire. For six years, he went broke trying to fund a dream. The only difference between him and us is he has decided to stay faithful to his purpose.

Joyce Meyer is another person I admire who had the strength to chase purpose. As a working mom, she felt God tell her that He wanted her to go into full-time ministry. This calling was a frightening thought for her because she had no clue how it would even begin. She also feared that her family would not be able to pay the bills, so she got a part-time job.

She tried to run from God's direct instruction. However, she was eventually fired from her part-time job. That's when she knew God meant business when He said he needed her to stay at home and focus on full-time ministry. So for the next six years, she studied the Word of God. She privately taught Bible study in her home and trusted God with her portion. Then one day, she got an invitation to fill in for a speaker who had canceled at a conference.

She placed her tapes on display, and everyone walked past them because they had no idea who she was. But, she was fortunate to present a five-minute invite/introduction to her workshop during the opening of the conference. The power of God that spoke to her that day filled the hearts of the people and her workshop the next day, quickly became standing room only. She didn't leave that conference with one single tape and just like that God had turned her preparation into purpose.

Discover Your Purpose

Please know that you don't have to be a minister or a famous person for God to use you. No matter what your interest is, God has designed a purpose for you. If you are on a job only because it provides you a really good income or gives you great clout in society, you're not chasing purpose, you're chasing paper.

Whether it's a crowd of millions, hundreds or even one-on-one, God has called you to show others His love.

Your purpose should draw others back to Christ. Whether it's a crowd of millions, hundreds or even one-on-one, God has called you to show others His love. It doesn't matter if you are a nurse, banker, teacher, chef, engineer or plumber, God has birthed a gift in you that gives you the ability to make a difference in someone's life every day. Don't be afraid of the gift you know that you have inside of you because of your fear of failure. Remember that the enemy binds people that he fears, so if you're struggling to release your God-given talent, it's because the enemy is afraid of the lives you will touch with your purpose. When trusting God to reveal my purpose there are few things I learned to do:

Learn to Dream

When I was in college I once had a friend ask me if I could do anything in world and money, where I lived and who I knew had no ability to hinder me, what would I do? I said an actress or some place in the movie business. Then I brushed it off as a silly dream as I was in school studying to be a psychologist. Most people who answer this question realize it's almost the complete opposite of what they are doing now. We tend to allow fear and others to cripple us from following our dreams. So if you can answer this question sincerely, you are one step closer to discovering your purpose.

Pray

Your next question should be why am I hungry for this dream? If you struggle with knowing if your next big idea for your life is a "God thing" versus a "good thing", then pray about it. When I accepted Christ, my only mandate in life became to draw others to Him. So if my dream doesn't seek to inspire, motivate or encourage others to believe in His love, then it's not a part of my purpose. I may be chasing a career, but if God isn't in the equation, I'm not chasing purpose.

Painful Moments

Some of our greatest blessings stem from our greatest disappointments. If I had never messed up in my relationships, I might have never tapped into the passion within me to encourage others to begin again. Tyler Perry said he started writing plays because he once heard Oprah say that writing was cathartic. He went through abuse as a child, and, therefore, he found his purpose by simply trying to find a way to release his inner pain. If you think something is worth fighting for, that fight within you is fueled by your passion for purpose.

Focus

Don't scatter yourself all over the place; focus on one thing at a time. I have been guilty of looking at famous media moguls like Steve Harvey, Tyler Perry, and Oprah Winfrey and immediately wanting to do everything that they are currently doing now. I swear, Steve Harvey has like ten different jobs. However, after reading their books and watching various interviews, they all say the same thing, figure out that one thing that you're good at and focus on that. Oprah started as an actress and then moved onto her talk show, Tyler Perry started with his plays and Steve Harvey started as a comedian. They all perfected these areas before branching into new ones. If you are patient enough, one day, all of your gifts will begin to take form right in front of you.

Stay in your Lane

The world would be a pretty dull place if we all wanted to do the same thing. Joyce Meyer tells a funny story of how she tried to run from her anointing by trying to be a 'normal' homemaker like her neighbor. Her neighbor was very good at gardening, and she thought that's what wives should do, so she did the same. During the harvest time, her neighbor's garden was beautiful and filled with crops, however, her garden next door didn't produce anything. She asked God how could this be? He told her I never told you to plant a garden, so I have no authority to bless it. If you have been watering a plant that will not grow, ask God if you are operating in your blessing or if you are simply out of His will. When you begin to walk into your unique God-given ministry, even if it's a ministry of gardening, God will make your plants grow!

Do the Work

I once had a young lady reach out to me to help her promote her new book. She had no money and didn't even know me personally but took a leap of faith to ask, to meet with me, so I said sure. I sat in the meeting brainstorming ideas with her, and then at the end of the meeting she said, "Great, when will you be able to do all of that?" I said, "I'm willing to help you, but I can't do all of the work." I told her the things I needed her to get in place so that I could get certain things in place for her, but I had to see her make the effort. After that meeting, the young lady never called me back. She may have gotten too busy, but whatever it was, she wasn't ready to put in the work, so the project went to the wayside. Yes, God will send people along the way to help us with our gift but if you are not prepared to invest in yourself, no one else will want to invest in you either.

You have to do your research, interviews, and attend conferences to enhance your gift. You have to position yourself for your blessing. You have to participate in your miracle. No matter how Hollywood tries to sell it, nobody is hardly ever a real 'overnight success.' I once heard Shonda Rhimes say in an interview, "Stop waiting for some big break and begin to prepare yourself now for the smaller breaks. If you are a writer, write every day until something happens." Work at your gift every day until something happens!

Sacrifice

Sometimes the journey to the path God has for you contain sacrifice. You can't take a shortcut; you have to grow through it!

The director of famous movie *Selma* said in an interview that we couldn't imagine the countless hours she spent in the mountains rewriting Dr. King's speeches to save her from copyright lawsuits. We have to be willing to go to a secluded place and let God speak to us. My time alone birthed *Sarah's Wedding*.

On your journey to your purpose you have to ask yourself, is what I'm about to do adding to my purpose or is it distracting me away from it?

It wasn't easy not dating, and it wasn't easy blocking out the world, traveling to my sister's house so that I could be alone and birth the purpose God had inside of me. Do you know how many times I wanted to break down, call my ex and ask him just to give me one more chance to make everything right? No matter how much I wanted to, I just couldn't. God was hiding me for a reason. I had to learn that until I was whole on my own, until I understood my purpose, I wouldn't have been any good to anyone. On your journey to your purpose you have to ask yourself, is what I'm about to do adding to my purpose or is it distracting me away from it? Is it a liability or an asset? Once you honestly answer that question, you will know what's worth sacrificing. I once read in Andy Stanley's book *The Principle of the Path* that you will always pay a price. However, it's up to you to decide whether you're going to pay now or pay later. I decided to pay now and let God prune me into my purpose rather than pay for never discovering my purpose later.

Have a Goal

Steven Covey says we must "begin with the end in mind". When you close your eyes, think of the moment that you want to experience and press towards it. If God gives you the vision, He will be faithful enough to complete it. Philippians 1:6 (NIV), "He who began a great work in you will be faithful to complete it in you."

Believe in Yourself

There are two quotes and one Scripture that I turn to whenever I begin to doubt the promises God has for me. "No matter where you come from your dreams are valid" - Lupita. Nyongo. "It doesn't matter who it's coming from, people support it, as long as it's good!" - Shonda Rhimes and Philippians 4:16 (NIV): "I can do all things through Christ who strengthens me." If you don't believe you are good enough, then nobody else will.

So what is your natural gift? I find joy in writing, speaking, hosting, producing, and event planning. However, all my gifts and talents expand from the gift of writing. It took me 28 years to realize my gift was a part of my purpose. God has promised that your gift will make room for you. So I dare you to start to chase the purpose within you!

Growth Exercise:

1. What do you feel is your God- given purpose?

2. List five specific things that you feel will help to develop your purpose?

Chapter 13

Courtship: Dating with a Purpose

After a whole year of not dating, I realized that I could no longer casually date. There were no more scales on my eyes and so even when I met someone I was physically attracted to, an alarm went off in my spirit when I saw a red flag. A lot times when we go on our very first date we see or hear the signs, but sometimes we choose to ignore them because it feels good to have someone to talk to again. In full transparency, there were still one or two times that my desires got the best of me, and I decided to proceed despite the red flags. However by the second or third date God snatched me back into His will, and I took heed to the signs. When you get to know you, you know so much quicker what you want in a relationship and what you don't. I don't want to date casually or just for fun. I want a courtship; I want to date God's way. I believe in dating with a purpose.

> I want a courtship; I want to date God's way.

One of the best things about dating God's way is the peace you have, knowing that you are in His will. In my past relationships, I had no peace because I wanted things to go my way. Every time I made a decision to go on a trip, have sex or forget to pray, my flesh was winning and Christ was losing. When you love someone or love the idea of having a relationship with someone, you don't care what Christ wants as long as you and your partner are happy. It's sounds harsh to say out loud, but it's true. Every time we make a decision to disobey God we are telling Him that we don't care what He wants. My one year challenge changed my mindset. I began to care what God thought about my love life and after a while certain things were no longer on the table. So I had to also learn to wait for someone with the same mindset.

There are a lot of people that want to date God's way but they choose not to because we tell ourselves that meeting someone with the same standards is impossible. We tell ourselves that kind of person simply doesn't exist. We tell God it's just not realistic to find someone who is also chasing purpose. Proverbs 18:21 (NIV) says that "life and death is in the power of the tongue" and, therefore, the more you speak negativity over your life the more you will believe it. Do you know how hard it is to see something that you don't even believe exists?

We love to blame not dating God's way on our lack of options, when in reality sometimes it's just us. We don't want to pray about every decision we make in our relationship and we don't want to give God permission to remove someone we love out of our life. For us it's just too much, so we tell God that we gave Him Sunday mornings and some Wednesday nights too, so isn't that enough to be considered dating "God's way"? When the truth is, if you are genuinely choosing to date God's way you are constantly choosing Christ's will over your mate's will and your will. It's a choice you have to make every day. It's scary to give God all of that authority because sometimes things may not happen, the way you wanted them to, but believe me when I say they will always happen the way you need them to.

I believe the difference between a Christ-centered courtship and casual dating is the choices that you make along the way. Therefore, if a Christ-centered marriage is your goal, then I believe choosing to date with a purpose is the path that will lead you there.

Pursuing vs. Waiting

Proverbs 18:22 (NIV), "He that findeth a wife findeth a good thing, and obtain the favor of the Lord". Ladies, according to Scripture you deserve to be pursued by a king. Gentlemen, you are called to pursue. Guys, this means you have to ask a female out on a date. The more time you spend making random small talk in fear that she will reject you, the weaker you will appear. And as the weeks pass, her confidence in your ability to lead her will begin to diminish. You are not asking for her hand in marriage by asking her on a date; you are simply asking to get to know her. Facebook chat and whats app messages are not a form of courtship, so make a decision to pursue and get to know her or make the decision to move on without her. As a man you are called to be the head, the leader, so simply just make a decision. The ball is in your court and its starts with you making the first shot.

Ladies, everyone is entitled to their opinion, and it may seem a little 'old school' but as the Scripture says, I strongly believe that I was called to wait. I believe it is a man's decision to make the request to court and my decision to accept or not accept. In a lot of relationships, I have heard friends say it's been three years, five years or even ten years, and he still won't commit to giving me a ring and I don't understand why. Well, I believe you get what you accept. Sometimes if a man knows you will wait five to ten years on him to make a decision, he will make you wait.

Secondly, I truly believe one of the reasons the guy is not taking the lead to ask you to be his wife is because he has never had to lead. If you asked him out on a first date, most likely he didn't make a decision, flattered by the ease of it all, he simply accepted. If you asked him to be exclusive or take your relationship to any other level, he didn't have to decide if he wanted to be serious about you, he simply followed your lead. So after years of never having to make a decision, you want him to know how to magically take the lead and make one! That's an unrealistic expectation, don't you think? The signs of his inability to lead were there from the start; you just chose to ignore them. Chances are if he's not leading you from the beginning, it's going to be hard for him to learn how to lead you later.

> I am willing to wait and follow a man who is being led by Christ.

I believe as women we were designed to wait to be led. It doesn't make me less of a woman to wait on a man, because when he approaches me I still have a decision to make. I can decide to pursue a relationship with him, or I can decide not to. After being in a relationship for years, I also have the right to make the decision to stay or to leave. I am willing to wait and follow a man who is being led by Christ. When Christ is his center, he knows himself and, therefore, knows what he wants. He knows that he was called to lead, and his decisions are on faith, not fear. That's the kind of man I am willing to wait for.

Standards vs. Picky

There is a difference between being picky and having standards. If you are counting a potential mate out because they are too short, too tall, too fat, light skin, dark skin, African descent, Caucasian, Asian, divorced, has a child or makes less money than you, all before getting to know them and their situation you are picky. If you prayed about it, and they don't have a solid relationship with God, different values from you, is married, wants to sleep with you, gets drunk in the club on the weekends and is spiritually weak, then I don't think you're picky; you are simply choosing to have standards.

As women, we sometimes get ourselves into problems because we refuse to date a man who makes less money than us, but will date a man who is still technically married to his wife, because he 'claims' the divorce is soon final. If you have to sin to get it, it's not a blessing from God. God will not send you somebody else's husband. So you have to choose if you want to pursue a relationship with standards or if you simply want to continue to be picky.

Having standards doesn't mean you are waiting for someone who is perfect; you are simply waiting for someone God created just perfectly for you. I use to get scared when I heard stories of women who found their mate and then said he wasn't my physical type. "I said what! Great! To date God's way I am required to date someone that I don't even feel an attraction to, how unfair is that?" However, the Holy Spirit eventually revealed to me that just because someone wasn't your original 'physical type' it doesn't mean you won't have an attraction to them.

I believe sometimes you do get someone who is your physical type, and sometimes you get someone you may have never considered before, but it's because you are looking with different eyes. When you choose to be picky when dating, you are looking for an attraction to the superficial, instead of being attracted to their purpose. I want to have a connection with my mate, and I believe God will honor that because I am open to an attraction based on standards and purpose.

Sobriety vs. Fantasy

Dating with purpose requires complete sobriety. As women sometimes after ten minutes of meeting someone who fits our 'checklist', we are halfway down the aisle, before even knowing his middle name. We must remember that our feelings are fickle, and, therefore, we cannot be controlled by our emotions. When we become wrapped up in a fantasy, we miss or ignore the signs that God wants us to see. We miss that he doesn't get along with his mother, has no clue where he sees himself in five years and has a serious fear of commitment.

Guys, you are not exempt either. Maybe you're not picking out wedding color pallets but sometimes you are thinking how great this girl will look on your arm or how much of a power couple you will be, instead of is she is truly a woman who possesses God-fearing qualities. Your physical attraction to her and your checklist that she fills out makes you blind to her manipulation, trust issues, and insecurity. The fantasies may be different for men and women, but no matter what fantasy you allow yourself to get caught up in, it still all lacks sobriety.

When you are sober, you watch someone's actions and not just their words. You take heed to their everyday values and not just their goals. You get to know who they are, not just who their 'representative' wants you to see. Dating with a purpose requires you to think about the hard questions that will reveal to you the true essence of their soul.

Values vs. Check List

I think anyone who has made the decision to be serious about dating has made a checklist, whether they physically wrote it down or kept it in their head. There are certain things we are simply looking for in a mate. I think the first time I wrote my checklist I had over 30 things on my list. Now, this may seem extensive to some but I was just trying to be honest with God. Over the years, I have decided to place more attention on my values and less on my checklist. It doesn't mean that I don't think a checklist is good. I think knowing what you want is good enough. However finding someone who simply had the values I was waiting for, seemed easier for me.

For me, values are important because they sit at the core of who I am. Knowing what you value is a good sign of knowing who you are. I believe you can sometimes ignore or overlook your values because you are so caught up in the honeymoon of the first two years of a relationship that you forget to bring the 'real you' to the table. I think marriage brings our values to a head and when they don't coincide with your spouse's values its chaos. And by that time it's too late. That's why I decided to be honest with myself about what was important to me and what wasn't, so that I could base my future relationships on my five values:

1.   A genuine relationship with God and obedience to His Word

2.   Family: An appreciation and love for immediate and extended

3.   Understanding, valuing and pursuing Purpose

4.   Growth: The desire to continue to learn and grow

5.   Health

Throughout the course of getting to know someone you begin to realize what values are important to them and what values are not. Finding someone who has over 30 things on your checklist may be impossible to find. Finding someone who has the same five values as you, makes you more open to meeting someone with whom you can share a solid foundation.

Romance vs. Sex

1 Corinthians 6:18 (NIV) says, "Flee from sexual immorality. Every other sin a person commits is outside the body, but the sexually immoral person sins against his body." As a Christian couple, we may stop going to the club, stop getting drunk on the weekends and we may even stop cursing, but we want God just to forget about the fact that He told us to flee sexual immorality. We tell God the flesh is too weak, and He's going to have to turn a blind eye. We will praise God during praise and worship and even cry during a powerful prayer but surrendering our sex life is often another story. However, until we are one in marriage as a

Christian couple, God will hold us accountable.

To avoid sex, we have to implement sexual boundaries, have accountability partners and older married couples as mentors. We have to surround ourselves with people we trust, people who will support and encourage us in a Christ-centered relationship. We also have to be well aware of our personal triggers. In Andy Stanley's sermon, he encourages couples to put off any kind physical activity as long as possible and to save sex for marriage. Founder of *Pinky Promise*, Heather Lindsay decided to wait to kiss until marriage. I think everyone's boundaries will be different. So it's up to you to pray about what's best for you.

In this prayer we need to be open and honest about how extreme our boundaries have to be. Whether it's no trips together, a curfew of 10 p.m., kissing only or group & public dates only, we have to learn to set boundaries. These boundaries will help us to remain sober in our decisions. Believe me when I say, there is nothing that clouds your judgment like a sexual relationship. Sex makes you forget the arguments, the pain and the stress of it all, and this is why God created it for marriage.

I choose Romance over Sex. Contrary to popular belief, romance isn't what you do so that you can have sex with someone. I believe romance should be used to get to know someone. Romance is a five hour conversation with someone stimulating your mind. It's uncontrollable laughter, words of encouragement, chivalry at dinner and gifts just because it's Thursday. Romance is the willingness to learn and speak your mate's love language; it's asking

THE ONE YEAR CHALLENGE

those 36 questions that the *New York Times* claims will help you fall in love.

Romance is listening to your mate even after they had a long day, holding their hand when they are scared and telling them how much you appreciate them. Romance is respecting and agreeing to wait because the person you're with is worth saving yourself for. I tried to choose sex over romance in the past and failed epically and so now I choose to wait.

God Thing vs. Good Thing

Have you ever heard someone say, "You two would go great together?" If I know the person and I have no chemistry, my reply is often "No, thanks!" There is nothing wrong with him, and trust me, if I say no, it's because I've already prayed, and I don't feel peace. It means that I have already tried the spirit, and I know it's not right. I have had many guys who I have partnered with in projects that have been simply amazing. And I know that the bond we shared is a bond that I would one day love to have with my future husband, but I want that and so much more. I can't miss out on that 'so much more' because I refused to be patient and wait on God's best for me. Sometimes people are simply in your life to teach you something new, give you a new perspective or just be a really good friend and that's ok. Every good guy isn't your guy! We can't allow the pressures of society to convince us just because someone has a lot of good qualities he or she must be the one for you! If you don't feel a peace about a connection, it's probably God telling you it's a good thing, not a God thing.

I believe you will know a God thing when you experience it. I once had a friend tell me the story of how she met her husband. She said she met him at a church picnic that she went to with her mom. When he approached her, she wasn't particularly interested because she didn't happen to believe good men exist. She was aloof and didn't think much their first interaction, but he was persistent. Every day he would send her nice messages, he would be a gentleman when they would go out, and they could talk for hours about any and everything. She still had her doubts, although, he didn't do anything wrong, she just knew that most guys eventually dropped the ball and assumed one day he would too. However, he was consistent. He never dropped the ball, their relationship wasn't perfect, but he was who he said he was, a man of God whom she loved. As the years went on, his consistency brought forth a ring and followed by a lovely wedding. She now enjoys marriage with the man who remained consistent. A God thing is not perfect, but it is full of peace. I think that's how you know it's a God thing and not just a good thing.

Giver vs. Taker

It wasn't until I was single that I realized I was a taker and not a giver. Of course, you do certain things for your significant other on birthdays and Christmas but doing those things doesn't make you a giver. That's simply fulfilling the bare minimum. Someone who is a giver will actively listen to your suggestion and strongly weigh out what's best for both of you. A taker will manipulate you into choosing what they want to do. A giver will offer to cancel plans for an event they want to attend, not because you asked but because they can hear in your voice how tired you are and that you may want to just head home to sleep, but a taker will ask what time should they be ready. A giver will cancel girls/guys night out to take care of you while you are sick. A taker will ask if you want them to pick up some soup and medication for you on the way home. If you can't be a giver in a dating relationship, then you won't know how to be a giver in marriage.

A marriage requires you to put your spouse needs over your own. It's like the book *100/0 Principle* by Al Ritter. Give 100% into a relationship and expect 0% in return. It sounds far-fetched, but I think that's what marriage is, going in prepared to give 100% even if you get nothing in return. It's like the movie *The War Room*. When she decided to stop focusing on all the things her husband did wrong and just focused on praying for their marriage, things began to change. She got a text message that her husband was at dinner with another woman, and yet she kept praying. The *100/0 Principle* says that even though this theory sounds strange, when you take the authentic responsibility for the relationship, more often than not, when you are persistent to give without expecting anything in return, the person often quickly chooses to take responsibility for the relationship as well. Eventually, the *100/0 Principle* turns into 100/100 because both people are focusing on giving and not taking. Every day I remind myself that I have to be a giver in my dating relationship if I want to be a giver in my marriage.

Faith vs. Fear

Jeremiah 29:11 (NIV) is one of my favorite scripture verses, "For I know the plans I have for you, declares the Lord. Plans to prosper you and not to harm you, plans to give you hope and a future."

When we genuinely believe in this verse, we choose faith over fear. Fear will make you believe that you have to settle for a relationship that does not reflect Christ's will. You make yourself believe the lie that this is as good as it's going to get, so you stay. Fear will cripple you from leaving an unhealthy relationship because the enemy tells you that you have invested too much time to leave now, you feel like a failure, so you convince yourself that things will get better once you or the person learns to change. You fear starting over or waiting on God's best because you don't believe or trust God's best plans for you. We get tired of waiting on God, so we try to help Him out. We make a decision to date our way and then when we get into trouble or pain, we ask God to bless and fix something He never gave us permission to put together. You won't be able to remove yourself from an unhealthy dating cycle until you realize that fear is only False Evidence Appearing Real.

Dating God's way requires faith, radical faith. I took over a year to begin this book because I didn't have radical faith. I worried about telling the world my story, and I worried about those who would arrive at the final chapter and begin turning the page with utter excitement in anticipation of my happily ever after. "Girl takes time away for God, girl gets rid of bad habits, girl gets to know herself, girl meets her King, and they live happily ever after, right?" Well, at least in my head that's how I wanted it to end, with a piece of evidence that would help others to believe doing it God's way was worth it. Well I'll let you get to Chapter 14 to see how it all ends, but I want you to remember when you give God the keys to your life, it may not always turn out the way you expected. Having faith isn't always easy, but when you choose Christ, He's not simply looking for you to give him the parts of you that you feel comfortable to give, He wants all of you. So I wrote my book in faith because sometimes God requires us to make the first step before he meets us halfway.

So when someone asks you what do you mean when you say that you are dating with a purpose, tell them that the purpose is a Christ-centered marriage. In a journey to courtship, marriage is the only goal. I want a Christ-centered marriage because in marriage when things get rough, you still have to make a choice to love that person every day. Even when that person is your least favorite person in the world, you have to remain faithful by continually making the decision to choose them. Well, that's all Christ wants. He wants us to practice being faithful. It's true, I hate choosing to be faithful to Christ sometimes because it's hard, but through the pain I know God has a great thing in store for me. So I choose to date God's way. I choose Faith over Fear!

Growth Exercise:

1. Write down three of your relationship standards, three ways that you can be a giver and three romantic gestures you can display in your current or future relationships.

2. What are your five personal Core Values?

Chapter 14
Partner
in Purpose

For decades, people have argued the existence of 'soul mates' or the 'one.' Asking the questions, "What if the person you were meant to marry marries someone else?" "What if the person you marry dies, and then you meet someone else, so who was the one, the one who died or the one you are married to now?" I honestly don't know the answer to these questions. What I do know is nothing God ever does is random. God has already ordained all of your days on this earth, so no matter what road we choose to travel, whatever is meant to be will be. Psalm 139:16 (NIV) tells us: "Your eyes saw my unformed body; all the days ordained for me were written in your book before one of them came to be."

I honestly believe the Scripture that teaches us that God knows our future before we even make a decision. It's true we have the choice to make whatever decision we want, but the amazing thing about God is, He already knows what choice you will make. Therefore I don't think it's up to us to figure out the logistics of how the 'one' exists, I think God just wants us to be open to His will for our life. I often tell people I want God's Plan A for my life. God gave me

> **The world needs something that only I have and the world is also waiting on something only you can give.**

free will, so I don't have to choose the path he's leading me toward, however, I want to choose it because I know that's God's greatest blessing for me lies on that path.

My purpose in life is specific and unique to me. There is no one else made on earth with my DNA for a reason. The world needs something that only I have and the world is also waiting on something only you can give. I won't be able to complete or fulfill my God-given purpose, if I don't marry someone who shares or supports the vision God gave me for my life and vice versa. That's why it's so important for us to discover our individual purpose before we enter into marriage. In the words of the late Dr. Myles Munroe, "When the purpose is unknown, abuse is inevitable." Knowing my purpose in life makes me whole, and if I'm not whole, I won't be able to give completely and purposely to a relationship or marriage. I will never be able to recognize, grow or prosper with my partner in purpose if I don't know what our purpose is together.

God created marriage as a ministry and in that ministry we both will have individual talents and gifts, but because we are one, there is something about those gifts and talents that will fulfill our God-given purpose together.

One of my favorite examples of a couple who discovered their purpose together is a young couple that I admire in the Turks and Caicos Islands. The wife is a dance instructor, and the husband is a basketball player. This couple had great dreams they wanted to build together, and with the help of God eventually their dreams became a reality. After a few years of entering marriage, they birthed their first brainchild *Little Ladies and Gents*; a kids multi-purpose facility which encompasses a kid's salon, barber shop, nail parlor, Learning Center, and Performing Arts school for dance and music all in one! This couple had a heart for children and their community in a major way, and because they understood their gifts, their passions and their purpose in life together they are successful. More importantly they supported and believed in one another. It was because of this they were able to make it all happen.

So when you think about a partner in purpose, I don't want you to think that you have to have the exact career or interest as your spouse. However, I do believe that you have to understand your individual purposes and have a vision from God on how those purposes can come together as one. If you want to do ministry overseas and your partner wants to have a traditional family life in their hometown, your purposes in life may not align. Therefore, it's important to have those hard conversations now.

One of my favorite messages on 'soul mates' or a partner in purpose, is from Pastor Toure Roberts, *The Five Keys to Identifying your Soulmate*. A soul mate question is a big question for a lot of people, and that is probably why his video became a You-Tube sensation. This sermon resonated with me on so many levels; I keep it in the back of my mind every time I meet someone new. I think if you are waiting for the person God chose for you to partner with in this life, this is a great list to use:

The Five Keys to Identifying your Soul Mate

1. **Chemistry** is the frequency you pick up when a certain person is around you.

2. **Connection** happens when you have a strong need or desire to be together

3. **Wholeness** qualifies the connection. When you're whole all on your own, before you meet the person

4. **A Word from God** involves a divine confirmation from God.

5. **A Sense of Purpose** is when you to feel a sense of purpose together.

Chemistry, Connection, Wholeness, A Word from God and A Sense of Purpose can all help to put your true desire for marriage into focus; however it all depends on the vision you want for your life. Some may ask, can I get married without following these guidelines and my answer is "of course you can." I just believe your marriage will be guaranteed to be purposeful when your choices are led by God. Pastor Toure isn't claiming to be an all-knowing 'love doctor' with these five steps, nor is he trying to say this is the only thing you need when identifying your purpose mate. He simply wanted to share a revelation of some essential things he felt God laid on his heart. And for me these five values are paramount.

Pastor Toure also used this sermon as an opportunity to talk candidly about how these five values led him to his first encounter with his soul mate. Their first date was actually the night before he launched his very first book "Purpose Awakening." He was busy in his purpose and just like that, God was writing his love story. This connection was so divine it didn't even take long to foster. A few months after their first date, Toure married this woman of God, the daughter of mega pastor, T.D. Jakes; Sarah Jakes. They both now live in Los Angeles, California where together they pastor *The One Church*. Since they have been married, they have flown all over the world fulfilling their purpose in ministry together. Their story serves as an encouragement to me that my partner in purpose is out there and that he is truly worth waiting for.

Worth the Wait

I believe that everyone's story is different, and so are our timelines. If you've never heard the song Worth the Wait by 33 Miles, and you are someone who has struggled with God's timing, I strongly encourage you to listen to it. One of my favorite lines says:

"It's worth the wait, just keep believing,

God has perfect timing, never early, never late,

it takes a little patience and a whole lot of faith,

but it's worth the wait. In His time, you will be fine;

all this waiting is by design."

God designed your life this way for a reason. I highlighted Sarah Jake's story in an early chapter but in case you forgot, here is a quick recap. Sarah had a baby by thirteen, was married by nineteen and divorced by twenty-two years old and yet God still introduced her to a new boo! So if nothing else, let this serve as a reminder to you, that there is nothing you have done that will disqualify you from God matching you with the one he has chosen for you.

I truly believe God will always fulfill his promises to you; your delay is not a denial. If God has promised it to you, it will surely come to pass. A few summers ago as I got ready to travel to Montreal for the first time, I realized at the last minute that I bought my ticket a day earlier than I needed to be there. I didn't have the money to spend on an extra night in the hotel, but I didn't have the money to change my ticket either, so I chose the lesser of two evils and decided to keep the same flight and pay for the extra night in the hotel. On the morning of the flight, I felt like I heard God say "You won't have to go to Montreal today." Being the frugal person that I am, I was very excited about this news. God was going to work it out, and I wouldn't have to waste any money by traveling a whole day early.

So when I arrived at the airport that morning I expected the agent to say something like, "The flight is full, would you mind going tomorrow?" or "The fight was cancel due to bad weather, you will have to fly out tomorrow." However, when I got to the ticketing counter, she said nothing. She simply checked me in and said to have a safe flight. I asked if the flight was on time, she said 'yup' and pointed me towards the back. Confused by it all, I thought to myself there I go again, thinking that I received some news from God when it was simply my selfish thinking. While waiting in the pre-boarding area, they told us that there would be a slight delay, but eventually we still boarded our flight. "Wow" I was wrong I thought to myself. I sat down in my seat on the plane and began to fall asleep. As I waited for us to take off, I couldn't stop fighting that glimmer of hope that I had in the fact that I heard from God. I battled with the doubt in my mind because what I was seeing was not what I felt I heard. Our plane engine had started, the doors were closed, and we were about to take off so maybe I was wrong.

It was about fifteen minutes after sitting on the runway God showed up. The plane had mechanical problems, and we would have to deplane. They told us to head back to the terminal to wait while they tried to fix the problem. About three hours later they called everyone with a connection to Montreal to the ticket agent counter and told us that we would have to stay one more night in the Bahamas because there was no way we would be able to catch our connecting flight to Montreal that day. There He was, right on time, five hours after check-in; God fulfilled His promise to me. I want to reassure you if God promised you something, no matter how far-fetched it may seem, or how long the wait, the Lord will provide His harvest for you.

I expected God to show up at the ticket counter, and then I expected Him to show up during the first delay. I started to give up on Him once I got on the plane; however my hope was restored once we were told to return to the terminal and even after that God, still made me continue to wait. Eventually after three more hours of waiting, God finally showed up. We may not always understand the wait, and we surely may not understand the timing but God is always on time. He designed your love story with a waiting period for a reason. God placed a word in my spirit that day and even when I doubted him, He still came through.

I can now truly say that the one year challenge was one of the best decisions I ever made. It taught me to trust God in the most unfathomable ways. That year and every year after have helped me to see what it meant to put Christ first. Matthew 6:33 (NIV) says, "Seek ye first the kingdom of God and all His righteousness will be given unto you." We can't control God's timeline for our lives, so when we choose to follow Him, we must simply be obedient to His will. I have comfort in knowing God will present my partner in purpose to me in His perfect timing, and I know he will be worth the wait.

So although I may not be where I had planned to be at this juncture in my life, I'm right where God needs me to be. These last few years have taught me that what Andy Stanley said in his series is true, "In real relationships happily ever after isn't about finding the right person. It's about becoming the right person." Before my one year challenge began, I was broken, rejected and defeated. God had to make me whole; He had to teach me a few lessons, and He had to grow my faith. God showed me how to love unconditionally, how to discover my purpose and His examples of true courtship. So you see, my one year challenge was never about finding the right guy; it was about finding me...

Growth Exercise:

1. Couples: Have a conversation with your partner/ spouse about how your purposes can align to fulfill your God-given purposes together?

2. Singles: Write down five things that you feel God has destined for your future that your future spouse should also be open to sharing or supporting?

ABOUT THE AUTHOR

KEREL PINDER is a writer, motivational speaker, television personality, producer and event planner. Kerel's mission in life is to inspire others to discover and flourish within their purpose by recognizing the importance of growth and a genuine relationship with God. Her vision in life is to not only make an impact within the Bahamas but to carry her passions throughout the entire world. Kerel's career as a Television personality & Host has afforded her opportunity to interview Bahamian celebrities, as well as Hollywood celebrities like Meagan Good and DeVon Franklin.

A citizen of the world but an island girl at heart; Kerel was born in the beautiful islands of the Bahamas. After High school, Kerel went on to obtain a Bachelor's Degree in Psychology from Acadia University and a Master's Degree in Education from the University of North Carolina, Chapel Hill. In December 2015 she obtained a second Master's degree in Communication and Leadership from Park University.

Kerel is also a former beauty queen, who has had the great privilege of representing her country nationally and internationally; competing as a beauty ambassador in China, Columbia, and the Philippines. In January 2016, Kerel added a new title to her resume by becoming a first-time author with the release of her book: "The One Year Challenge – A new Journey to Love, Purpose & Courtship."

Kerel is open to local and international speaking engagements and book signing events; these requests should be directed to www.kerelpinder.com. You can follow Kerel on Twitter at @kerelpinder or like her on Facebook at KerelPinder. She can also be found on Instagram at @kerelpinder1908

The ONE YEAR Challenge

A new journey towards
LOVE, PURPOSE & COURTSHIP

KEREL R. PINDER

Made in the USA
Lexington, KY
07 March 2016